Islāmically Modified Cognitive Behavioural Therapy

This book outlines the methods and practice of Islāmically Modified Cognitive Behavioural Therapy (IMCBT), a modified version of CBT adapted to the Muslim client's preferences, culture, and religion.

The book begins by establishing IMCBT's fidelity to the core competencies and evidence-based practices of CBT while also introducing new unique features and interventions related to Muslim clients. It uses real-life cases to offer practical strategies for overcoming stigma, forming the therapeutic alliance, structuring the session, and utilising the client's faith for coping and problem-solving. Chapters comprehensively provide CBT skills competencies with Islāmic modifications for a range of topics including case conceptualisation, reframing, cognitive restructuring, and advanced coping strategies for addressing interpersonal conflicts and enhancing therapeutic outcomes. The book also offers both proscriptive and prescriptive ethical guidance by showcasing instances where clients experienced negative outcomes with other practitioners to emphasise the dangers of not properly preparing for and understanding how to work with Muslims who prioritise their faith.

This book will appeal to practitioners, educators, and students who are seeking deeper ways of adapting their practice, teaching, or learning to the Muslim client's needs while also maintaining fidelity to the core features of CBT.

Mahdi Qasqas, MACP, PhD (in Social Work), is the head Psychologist at Q&A Psychological Services, supervising practicum students and provisional psychologists. Moreover, he is a researcher and consultant and provides training in Psycho-Spiritual First Aid® to lay helpers, clergy, and health professionals.

Focus Series on Islāmic Psychology
Series Editor: Professor Dr. G. Hussein Rassool, Professor of Islāmic Psychology.

About the Series

In contemporary times, there is increasing focus on the need to adapt approaches of psychology, counselling psychology and psychotherapy to accommodate the integration of spirituality and psychology. With the increasing focus on the need to meet the wholistic needs of Muslims, there was a call to adapt approaches to the understanding of behaviour and experiences from an Islāmic epistemological and ontological worldview.

The aim of the Focus Series on Islāmic psychology and psychotherapy is to introduce a range of educational, clinical and research interventions relating to Islāmic psychology and psychotherapy that are authentic, practical, concise, and based on cutting-edge research. Each volume focuses on a particular aspect of Islāmic psychology and psychotherapy, its application with a specific client group, a particular methodology or approach, or a critical analysis of existing and emergent theoretical and historical ideas.

Each book in the Focus Series is written, in accessible language, with the assumption that the readers have no prior knowledge of Islāmic psychology and psychotherapy.

Integrated Research Methodologies in Islāmic Psychology (2024)
G. Hussein Rassool

Integrating Acceptance and Commitment Therapy with Islamic Psychotherapy for Managing Chronic Pain (2024)
Razia Bhatti-Ali

Integrating Spiritual Interventions in Islāmic Psychology
A Practical Guide (2024)
Juraida Latif, Shaakirah Dockrat Boda, & G. Hussein Rassool

Islāmically Modified Cognitive Behavioural Therapy (2025)
Mahdi Qasqas

Islāmically Modified Cognitive Behavioural Therapy

Mahdi Qasqas

Routledge
Taylor & Francis Group
LONDON AND NEW YORK

Designed cover image: © Getty Images

First published 2024
by Routledge
4 Park Square, Milton Park, Abingdon, Oxon OX14 4RN

and by Routledge
605 Third Avenue, New York, NY 10158

Routledge is an imprint of the Taylor & Francis Group, an informa business

British Library Cataloguing-in-Publication Data
A catalogue record for this book is available from the British Library

ISBN: 978-1-032-42765-2 (hbk)
ISBN: 978-1-032-42767-6 (pbk)
ISBN: 978-1-003-36420-7 (ebk)

DOI: 10.4324/9781003364207

Typeset in Times New Roman
by Apex CoVantage, LLC

To my mother, then my mother, then my mother, then my father.

Contents

Acknowledgements

I would like to express my sincere gratitude to Ayesha Notiar for her invaluable assistance, as well as to all of my students. I would also like to extend my heartfelt appreciation to Professor Dr G. Hussein Rassool for his leadership as the Focus Series Editor and his constructive feedback in getting this book to its final polished form.

Preface

Bayan: If it weren't for my *deen* (*Islām*), I would have killed myself.
Mahdi: It sounds like your faith is literally saving your life.

Religion and spirituality can certainly be powerful forces to help people get through and bounce back from some of life's most difficult challenges. For Bayan, and many others I have worked with over the last 20 years, it plays a significant role in their lives. Imagine if the response to the client whose faith serves as a protective measure against suicide was "Maybe your faith is the problem". Although I doubt any competent and ethical therapist would ever do this, sometimes the lack of understanding can lead to missed opportunities, cause irreparable damage to the therapeutic alliance, or lead to premature termination.

Adam: I have to pray.
Therapist: Maybe that's the problem.

This exchange actually took place with someone I know dearly which led to premature termination. However, the therapist could have seamlessly reframed her concern in a variety of ways and used the client's prayer to restructure the therapeutic relationship and goals. That is, Islāmic practices can be a wealthy source of motivation and be used to enhance client engagement and make better use of evidence-based therapeutic interventions. What if, instead, the therapist said:

Therapist: What if we used psychological principles and techniques to help you with praying on time and developing more concentration in prayer? Would that be a meaningful use of our time together?

How do you think this client would respond? To add some context, he is a devout Muslim who, despite Islām being a priority in his life, is perhaps struggling to maintain his prayers on time and thus often feels pressured to get up and pray before the time runs out; a challenge faced by many Muslims. How could using the prayer to facilitate time management and mindfulness likely change the trajectory of therapy and perhaps his life? Can it serve to simultaneously enhance his mental and spiritual health and well-being? In short, if mental health professionals are able to adapt their therapeutic approach to the client's preferences, culture, and religion, they would not only be operating from a highly ethical and evidence-based practice standpoint, but they would also likely enhance positive therapeutic outcomes with their clients. In this book, a range of examples are provided on how to Islāmically modify cognitive behavioural therapy using Islāmic principles, practices, and teachings. Although there is no one right way of doing therapy, there is certainly a wrong way.

Therapist: I want you to just turn off your mind and not think or do anything while you are lying in bed.
Naimah: I can't, I have to do my prayers before sleeping.
Therapist: Can't you just put your religion aside for once?

Although the challenges and missed opportunities will be more detailed when discussing evidence-based practices (what works and what does not work in therapy), this transcript could more aptly be titled "how to ruin your relationship with your Muslim client while subsequently violating your own ethical principles and neglecting evidence based practice". It is one thing to make a slight error of omission, but to ignore both science and ethics is likely to not only cause irreparable damage to the client but also place the discipline in disrepute. Asking the client to put aside something so important to her is akin to saying, "I don't care about your opinion, I know what's best for you, so just do it" and is often the antithesis of how therapy works. However, there is more to this one instance in therapy than meets the eye. First, imagine how it feels to be stressed out and someone says, "just relax". Or to feel depressed and someone says, "just cheer up". Or to be suffering from any type of pain and be met with the words, "be grateful for what you have, others have it way worse". These can be referred to as toxic positivity, prescribing the outcome, and many more dysfunctional ways of inadvertently (and quite likely unintentionally) telling someone, "I don't really care about your problem, I just want to avoid the feeling of not knowing what to say or do".

Toxic positivity and imposing a structured application of an intervention without considering the client's context can be associated with spiritual shaming and other forms of emotional suppression that can be more harmful to the client's mental and spiritual health and well-being; even if it is an empirically supported intervention. One key point that I try to make in this book is that despite the power that integrating faith and spirituality into therapy can have, it can also come with a high degree of risk if it is not done judiciously. Thus,

I introduce some guiding principles and themes that are essential in the development and conceptualisation of Islāmically Modified Cognitive Behavioural Therapy (IMCBT) and can facilitate a more ethical and evidence-based approach to research and working with Muslims.

Another essential feature in this book is the importance of applying a rigorous and systematic process of ensuring that the Islāmic content used is considered to be credible by Islāmic scholars. During a supervision session with two of my students, I asked them what evidence means. One of the students quickly responded with "data and research". However, I wanted to challenge their thinking to enhance their cognitive development and encourage a broader perspective. So I asked two questions that I find to be essential knowledge when integrating Islām into psychotherapy. Since the essential bodies of knowledge are the Qur'ân and *sunnah*, I first asked, "is there a difference in the quality of evidence to support the authenticity of a Hadīth?". They concurred and were aware of the different classifications of Hadīth.

Although there is a lack of meta-analyses of randomised controlled trials on Muslims, in my approach to developing IMCBT, I chose not to rely on descriptive studies as foundational support. Instead, I drew inspiration from the Islāmic perspective on the distinction between weak and strong Hadīth. According to this perspective, weak Hadīth can be used in certain contexts (usually in historical accounts or encouraging good behaviours), but they should not be used to establish fundamental principles. Similarly, while descriptive research or case studies may provide interesting narratives or insights, I recognised the importance of utilising robust evidence, such as meta-analyses of randomised controlled trials, to establish the foundational principles of this therapeutic model. By following this approach, I aimed to uphold the scholarly rigour and reliability required to develop a credible and effective framework.

The second question was, "is there a systematic process to tafsir/exegesis or interpretation of the Qur'ân?". They responded in the affirmative but did not know the methodology behind how it was done. This was enough to make the argument that in Islām, we have a systematic method of analysing evidence that predates the field of psychology, just as we also have counselling strategies that predates the English language. Against this backdrop, this approach was developed, and this book was written. IMCBT is thus conceptualised as a culturally adapted and localised clinical application of CBT guided by a set of guiding principles and themes to enhance its credibility. The hypothesis is that the degree of credibility of IMCBT is predicated on the principles of fidelity and flexibility. In the context of this book, it would be fidelity to the evidence, core principles, and practices of both entities – Islām and CBT.

Structure of the Book

Part I of this book focuses on laying the foundation for IMCBT. One purpose for writing this book is to help students and other types of knowledge seekers understand the core functional and foundational competencies that are expected of psychologists while also demonstrating how IMCBT meets such standards. However, I believe it is important for students to first develop a solid foundation in evidence-based practices and empirically supported treatments before learning to adapt to the client's culture, preferences, religion, stages of change, and other important factors associated with therapeutic outcomes.

Thus, in Chapter 1, the structural foundations of CBT are introduced along with a summary of the best available evidence that spans all therapies summarised in my CARE in the CHAIR model. The guiding principles and themes employed to develop and practise IMCBT are also covered. In Chapter 2, I provide a brief overview of the perspectives and discourses in the field of Islāmic psychology and posit a fourth approach – the convert approach. I use this analogy to position IMCBT as being a grandchild with a secular behavioural and cognitive psychology heritage and has more compatibility with CBT than "we think" (which serves as a double entendre or double meaning). In Chapter 3, I introduce you to Mr Shakib, who started therapy with the belief that mental health is a sin or forbidden. This chapter moreover provides a discussion on barriers and some practical ways of navigating stigma, uncertainty, and anxiety. In Chapter 4, I examine the top criticisms against CBT and explain how the underlying logical fallacy used can also be seen in misconceptions and criticisms against Islām; reaffirming the importance of using evidence to make informed judgements and decisions.

In Part II, I focus on the core knowledge and skills competencies required for practising CBT, along with Islāmic modifications and evidence-based malpractice or what does not work in therapy. In Chapter 5, I provide the Islāmic correlates to core CBT knowledge competencies, which include an understanding of the theoretical underpinnings related to both pathology and change mechanisms. In Chapter 6, the core CBT skills competencies are comprehensively listed, and Islāmic modifications are discussed. In Chapter 7, I introduce you to Naimah, a client of mine who had the unfortunate (and preventable) experience of being told to put her faith aside. This chapter should be consulted if you want to know what not to do in therapy with any client, not just a Muslim one.

Part III focuses on practice with an emphasis on clinical application. In Chapter 8, I share a structured way of opening the session with Muslims who respond to most enquiries about how they are feeling or doing with a very common phrase – *alhamdulillah* (All praise is due to Allāh). Describing a real-case scenario in therapy in writing inevitably falls short of capturing the full depth and complexity of the experience. Written words can convey only a fraction of the nuances, non-verbal cues, and emotional intricacies present in an actual session. This is especially true when I explain the use of humour in therapy in Chapter 9. Chapter 10 reviews case conceptualisation as an essential competency to possess and how it can be enhanced with Islāmic modifications. In Chapter 11, I put forth a brief overview of my Islāmically integrated ethical and practice framework called *akhlaq* minus *nifaq* (characteristics minus hypocrisy) to explain some essential Islāmic life values and provide how it was also applied as an intervention with Saleema. Chapter 12 provides an analysis of the case where Adam's therapist could have used prayer as an opportunity for his growth and development but, instead, perhaps focused more on maintaining their manualised approach to CBT. I also bring Saleh into the discussion to provide a recommended approach to a very common issue. In Chapter 13, we delve into the use of *dua* or supplication interventions as a powerful tool to address an interpersonal conflict Malik has been having with his wife and demonstrating how negative and intrusive thoughts can be simultaneously addressed from an Islāmic and CBT approach while still being credible to both worldviews. Chapter 14 covers Islāmically modified coping strategies and provides a deeper look at commonly used interventions and potential alternatives to the existing religious CBT. Chapter 15 brings us to the end of our journey with a conclusion and some possible future applications of IMCBT.

A Final Note on the Client Cases and Islāmic Evidence

Throughout this book I will be using real-life cases, which I believe can provide a higher degree of credibility. Thus, each of the cases included is from actual cases I have personally worked with. Although the names are all pseudonyms and all identifying information is purposefully removed, most of the names were intentionally chosen based on the presenting concern of the client. For example, Mr Shakib presents quite anxiously as he asks, "Isn't mental health *haram* (forbidden)". Furthermore, he was referred for an anxiety-related disorder. The connection between anxiety and uncertainty is one that I often endorse in the cognitive formulation of such problems. The Arabic term *shak* can mean doubt or uncertainty, and, thus, despite being a typical Pakistani name, Shakib is not Pakistani.

The inspiration to pay attention to such details comes from my personal experience and can be grounded in reader-response theory. Reader-response theory (Tompkins, 1980; Beach, 1993) is a literary approach highlighting the reader's active role in interpreting a text. Thus, rather than focusing only on my intentions, I wrote this book acknowledging how your personal experience, emotions, and reactions might be and being careful to respect your sensibilities; even if I have no way of knowing or guaranteeing what they might be. Thus, in all of the cases I put forth, I tried to focus mainly on the key presenting concern to avoid cultural misappropriations and hopefully enhance credibility (or prevent rejection) through an application of reader-response theory. What I also aimed to do is try to utilise the "unifying cultural elements" (Haque & Keshavarzi, 2014, 298) found in Islām.

To ensure that I maintained a high degree of fidelity to Islāmic evidence, I consulted local scholars on each modification. For example, the following Hadīth was subjected to a series of inquiries to ensure crediblity in the conclusion. "Every disease has a cure. If a cure is applied to the disease, it is relieved by the permission of Allāh Almighty" (Muslim (a)). Before finalising this intervention, I raised critical questions to ensure a proper conceptual understanding. Querying, can the term "disease" be replaced with "problem" without altering the Hadīth's essence? Can "cure" be substituted with "solution" while preserving the intended meaning? Furthermore, does matching the right problem with the right solution align with the conceptual understanding of this Hadīth? While scholars consulted provided affirmative responses, readers are encouraged to consult their own local scholars to ensure an authentic application of this understanding.

Despite some chapters seeming a little heavier with Islāmic concepts and principles, it should not lead you to ever feel discouraged or in any way think that you cannot integrate Islām at such a deep level. That is, assuming you find the material credible and by extension, likely to follow up on it through your own professional development. However, if such feelings do arise at any point while reading this book, I encourage you to use some basic CBT interventions to manage your own thoughts (e.g. "it is too hard") and feelings resulting in possible avoidance behaviour. To do this, you would first need to know that there is no evidence to support that you cannot master these skills, but rather there is ample evidence to support that you have, once upon a time, been in a similar situation of developing your competence. Furthermore, gradual progress is key to any change process, and change can be seen when we commit to consistent actions, even if small. A negative coping style here would likely be full of logical fallacies and lead to avoidance or other dysfunctional behaviours. Thus, I encourage you to read this book first and foremost for yourself, to facilitate whatever journey you are on, and I pray that you can walk away with knowledge that benefits yourself and those you will undoubtedly help in the near or distant future.

Glossary

Page	*Transliterated Arabic*	*Arabic Script*	*English*
5	*deen*	الدين	*religion/way of life*
	alhumdulilah	الحمد لله	*All praise is due to Allah*
	akhlaq	أخلاق	*positive attitudes, behaviours, and characteristics*
	nifaq	نفاق	*hypocrisy*
	haram	حرام	*forbidden*
	shak	شك	*doubt*
	Chapter 1	الفصل الأول	
	Islām	إسلام	*(peace acquired as a result of) submission*
	Islāmic	إسلامي	*pertaining to Islām*
	Islāmicise	أسلمة	*to make something Islāmic*
	Sunni	سني	*Way (of the way [of the Prophet PBUH])*
	aHadīth	أحاديث	*narrations*
	tafsir	تفسير	*exegesis*
	sufi	صوفي	*Sufi*
	Chapter 2	الفصل الثاني	
	tawhîd	توحيد	*monotheism (Singling Allah in worship)*
	sunnah	سنة	*way*
	taddabur	تدابر	*reflection*
	hikmah	حكمة	*wisdom*
	Chapter 3	الفصل الثالث	
	haram	حرام	*forbidden*
	majnoon	مجنون	*insane*
	huzn	حزن	*sorrow*
	gham	غم	*worry*
	ham	هم	*stress*
	ghayth	غيث	*anger*
	ya's	يأس	*hopelessness*
	fatwa	فتوى	*religious ruling*
	hukm	حكم	*general law*

(*Continued*)

(Continued)

Page	Transliterated Arabic	Arabic Script	English
	dhikr	ذكر	*remembrance*
	alhumdulilah	الحمد لله	*All praise is due to Allah*
	Chapter 4	الفصل الرابع	
	iman	إيمان	*faith*
	Chapter 5	الفصل الخامس	
	shahawat	شهوات	*desires*
	maqasid	مقاصد	*objectives*
	shariah	شريعة	*Islāmic law*
	ahkam	أحكام	*rules/laws*
	haram	حرام	forbidden resulting in sin by commission
	makrooh	مكروه	disliked – but no sin by commission but reward for omission
	mubah	مباح	permissible – neither sinful nor rewarded
	mustahab	مستحب	encouraged – no sin for omission but reward for commission
	wajib	واجب	obligatory – reward for commission and sin for omission
	Chapter 6	الفصل السادس	
	shaytan	شيطان	*devil*
87	*dhikr or thikr?*	ذكر	*Remembrance (of Allah)*
	QaddarAllāh, wa ma sha'a fa'al	قدر الله وما شاء فعل	It is the decree of Allāh and what He wills He does
	mashallah	ما شاء الله	*What Allah wills*
	mushrikeen	مشركين	*polytheists*
	talbiyah	تلبية	
	subhanAllāh	سبحان الله	*Far exalted is Allah from what they associate with Him*
	Chapter 7	الفصل السابع	
	Islām	إسلام	*(peace acquired through) submission*
	Quran	قرآن	*recitation*
	thikr	ذك	*remembrance*
	Chapter 8	الفصل الثامن	
	Muslim	مسلم	*person who submits to Allah*
	Salamu Aleykum	السلام عليكم	*Peace be upon you*
	Islām	إسلام	*(peace acquired through) submission*
	ﷺ		*May the peace and blessings of Allah be upon him (Prophet Mohammed)*
	Allah	الله	*The God*

(*Continued*)

(Continued)

Page	Transliterated Arabic	Arabic Script	English
	Bukhari	البخاري	*the biggest collection of narrations*
	Islāmic	إسلامي	*pertaining to Islām*
	sallam	سلام	*peace*
	Chapter 9	الفصل التاسع	
	Shoo, ana mish majnoonah	ماذا؟ أنا غير(مش) مجنونة	*what, I am not crazy*
	Aywa	أيوا	*AH-HA*
	Sallamu Alaykum, Alhamdulillah ala Al Salamah	السلام عليكم الحمد لله على السلامة	*A colloquial phrase literally translated as Thank God for your safety but means a lot more.*
	Alhamdulillah Ala al Khayr wal Shar	الحمد لله على الخير والشر	*This is a statement that reflects the fundamental belief of Muslims related to fate and destiny and is translated as Thank God for the Good and the Bad*
	Hatti al Shar	أعطني الشر	*Give me the Bad*
	khayr	خير	*good*
	shar	شر	*bad*
	Chapter 10	الفصل العاشر	
	deen	دين	*faith*
	aqeedah	عقيدة	*Islāmic creed*
	Aamaal al quloob, lisan, and jawarih	أمل القلوب، إسلام،الجوارح	*actions of the heart, tongue, and limbs*
	ﷺ		*May the peace and blessings of Allah be upon him (Prophet Mohammed)*
	aamal	أمل	*actions*
	silah	سلاح	*connectedness or choice*
	Chapter 11		
	qabool	القبول	
	salaam	سلام	*peace*
	taaruf	تعارف	*understanding*
	shura	شورى	*mutual consultation*
	ikhras	إخرس	*be quiet*
	sid thummak	أغلق فمك	*shut your mouth*
	akhlak bidoon nifaq	أخلاق بدون نفاق	*characteristics without hypocrisy*
	awliya	أولياء	*saints*
	subhanAllāh	سبحان الله	
	husnul than	حسن الظن	*positive and rational opinions*
	sabr	الصبر	*patience*
	nadm	الندم	*guilt*
	mithali	مثالي	*ideal*
	La yukalifullahu	لا يخالف الله	*Allāh does not test a person*
	illa wus3aha	إلا ويخشاه	*except what it can bear*

(*Continued*)

(Continued)

Page	*Transliterated Arabic*	*Arabic Script*	*English*
	Chapter 12	الفصل الثاني عشر	
	Tahfeez programme	تحفيظ برنامج	
	ilm	علم	*knowledge*
	yaqeen	يقين	*certainty*
	qabool	قبول	*acceptance*
	inqiyad	انقياد	*submission*
	sidq	صدق	*truthfulness*
	ikhlas	إخلاص	*sincerity*
	muhabbah	محبة	*love*
	fajr	فجر	*morning prayer*
	qadda	قادة	*making up the prayer*
	Al-iman yazeed wa yankus	ألإيمان يزيد وينقص	*faith increases and decreases*
	shuyukh	شيوخ	
	Ansar	أنصار	
	niyyah	نية	*intention*
	JazakAllāh u Khayr	جزاك الله خيرا	
	Chapter 13	الفصل الثالث عشر	
	dua	دعاء	*supplication*
	waswasa	وسوسة	*whispers from the devil*
	shyateen	شياطين	*devils*
	Authoobillahi minal shaytan al rajeem	أعوذ بالله من الشيطان الرجيم	*I seek refuge in Allāh from the accursed satan*
	istiaathah	استغاثه	*seeking refuge in Allāh from the whispers of the devils*
	Shukr	شكر	*gratitude*
	Iyyakum wal law?	إياكم والكذب	*Beware of why*
	jin	جن	*demon*
	Chapter 14	الفصل الرابع عشر	
	khayr	خير	*good*
	ahsanul than bilnaas		Have *husnul than* or positive opinions of people)
	taddabur	تدبر	*deep reflection*
	yaqeen	يقين	*certainty*
	iman	إيمان	*faith*
	tawbah	توبة	*repentance*

Part I

Foundations

1 Introduction to Islāmically Modified Cognitive Behavioural Therapy

Islāmically Modified CBT (IMCBT) is conceptualised as a culturally adapted and localised clinical application of CBT guided by a set of guiding principles and themes to enhance its credibility.

Cognitive behavioural therapy (CBT) celebrates a high degree of credibility as being one of the most widely studied families of evidence-based practices and empirically supported treatments used by mental health professionals (Fordham et al., 2021). It has been especially effective in treating a wide range of disorders listed in the fifth edition of the *Diagnostic and Statistical Manual of Mental Disorders* (DSM 5), especially major depressive disorders (Cuijpers et al., 2023). Thus, it makes sense that CBT is also one of the most culturally adapted interventions (Rathod et al., 2018) that demonstrate the added benefit of modifying certain features. That is, culturally adapted and religiously adapted versions of CBT have also received a great deal of empirical support with scholarly calls to continue to develop CBT interventions to be more relevant and responsive to diverse populations and new challenges (Hall, Ibaraki, Huang, Marti, & Stice, 2016; de Abreu Costa & Moreira-Almeida, 2022). Thus, IMCBT can be viewed as a culturally or religiously adapted version of CBT; but there is certainly more to it.

Structure

CBT is a therapy that belongs to the specialisation of behavioural and cognitive psychology. A specialty is a defined area of professional psychology practice characterised by a distinctive configuration of competent services for specified problems and populations (American Psychological Association, 2020, p. 2).

There are also shared core knowledge and skills competencies that the sub-areas of a specialty should all have in common (Klepac et al., 2012) and will be detailed later on in this book. The sub-areas of a specialty area can be grouped based on their shared theoretical foundations and approaches towards

DOI: 10.4324/9781003364207-2

case conceptualisation. That is, truly innovative and new ideas in therapy are rare, however, this does not exclude the usefulness of developing and committing to a specific construct.

Thus, Islāmically modified therapies need not be innovative to the extent that they develop new theories and ideas but rather their commitment and enhancement of certain constructs. What tends to differentiate therapies is the emphasis placed on either populations served, problems addressed, settings, or procedures used (Rodolfa et al., 2005). For example, behaviour therapy, cognitive behaviour therapy, and cognitive therapy all belong to the family of cognitive and behavioural psychology, as they all share a foundation in learning and behaviour theories as well as how case conceptualisation is usually approached. Furthermore, Acceptance and Commitment Therapy and Problem-Solving Therapy are also part of this family. There are also versions of CBT that target specific challenges such as CBT for Insomnia (CBT-I) and others that emphasise specific aspects but retain the theoretical foundation like Dialectical Behavioural Therapy (DBT) and more recently, Judith Beck's recovery-oriented CBT (CT-R). CT-R retains its theoretical underpinning in CBT but "Rather than emphasising symptoms and psychopathology, CT-R emphasises clients' strengths, personal qualities, skills, and resources" (Beck, 2021, p. 7).

The same can be said for most of the newer therapies that have a foundation in behavioural and cognitive psychology. Likewise, IMCBT also retains the theoretical foundation of the cognitive model, with an emphasis on being culturally adapted and localised to a Muslim client. Since CBT already requires a sound therapeutic relationship, is culturally adapted, and tailored to the individual (Beck, 2021), what can make IMCBT truly unique is not just its emphasis on Muslims but also its guiding principles and themes, which can be extended to other populations. However, rather than just stating my opinion on IMCBT, I will aim to demonstrate its credibility. The hypothesis here is that the degree of credibility of IMCBT is predicated on the quality of the evidence used from both the scientific and Islāmic scholarly communities in the modifications and applications of core CBT interventions. It is against this backdrop that IMCBT is developed to enhance its credibility through the fidelity pathway. Fidelity and flexibility are guiding principles that serve to enhance credibility. In the context of this book, it would be fidelity to the evidence, core principles, and practices of both entities – Islām and CBT.

Credibility

To guide this process of establishing credibility, I start by using what I call the "Beginning with the Best in Mind Principle". This guiding principle helps with setting a high standard from the onset and working to ensure that fidelity to the principles and values of those I aim to serve (my guests and students) and represent (my community and profession) can be transparent.

Academically speaking, being accepted by two epistemic communities (e.g. Islām and psychology) as credible is the ultimate objective. This approach is also highly relevant to a core foundational competency in health service psychology related to interdisciplinary practice (Fouad et al., 2009). In particular, having knowledge of the "key issues and concepts in related disciplines" (p. S15). This goes beyond just knowing the definitions but also having respect and valuing the shared and unique contributions of different professions.

This guiding principle also helps with the often-complicated process of choosing definitions and sources of evidence. Although I reviewed everything I could get my hands on, I realised, instead of trying to sift through thousands of books and articles on CBT for a consensus of definitions and principles, I chose instead to select from what is assumed to be the highest source of authority on psychology in the Western hemisphere – the American Psychological Association (APA). In particular, I derived the core foundational and functional competencies established by this association. The APA serves as the governing body that accredits institutions to provide the core educational requirements to practise as a psychologist in most of the Western world. Although this point can be argued (especially if decolonisation is to be discussed), it does provide a reliable and publicly available source for you to consult and critique as you judge the credibility of IMCBT.

Credibility and Psychology

Behavioural and cognitive psychology is a specialty area identified by the APA, the Council of Specialties in Professional Psychology, and the American Board of Professional Psychology. Any institution would need to consult the core principles and processes of the specialisation if it is to be accredited. A document outlining these features exists for every specialisation; for example, these guidelines are published by the inter-organisational task force on cognitive and behavioural psychology doctoral education (Klepac et al., 2012). Thus, in my opinion, this was the best place to begin from to develop and evaluate how credible IMCBT would be to CBT scholars and practitioners; even if you are not (or do not plan on being) a doctoral student. This process included first looking at all the documents that the inter-organisational task force used to identify its core competencies. That is, tracing the evidence back to the original source is also in line with beginning with the best in mind.

Core Foundational and Functional Competencies

Shifting to competency-based training has become the new normal for graduate programmes in the professional practice of psychology as a health service (Fuertes, Spokane, & Holloway, 2012). The competencies are often described in terms of benchmarks and behavioural indicators and located in a document outlining the taxonomy. Two current models are dependent on for any specialisation (including behavioural and cognitive psychology), with respect to competency in health service psychology. Mainly, Fouad et al.'s (2009) competency benchmarks, which are built on the foundations set in Rodolfa et al.'s (2005) Competencies Cube. The decision of the competency benchmark workgroup was based on the credibility of the Cube model as being "widely cited and recognised as credible at this point in the evolution of competency-based education and training" (Fouad et al., 2009, p. S8).

In Fouad et al. (2009), the competency benchmarks list the behavioural anchors of each of the core foundational and functional competencies across three stages of readiness and professional development, namely readiness for practicum, internship, and entry to professional practice. Although these terms may have different meanings in different locations they still represent the normal trajectory students progress through (e.g. in my province, these three would align with practicum student, provisional psychologist, and then psychologist).

The comprehensive list of foundational competencies includes reflective practice and self-assessment, scientific knowledge and methods, relationships, ethical and legal standards and policy issues, individual and cultural diversity, and interdisciplinary systems. Each of these could intersect with functional competencies which include assessment, diagnosis, conceptualisation, intervention, research, evaluation, consultation, supervision, teaching, management, and administration. Thus, if IMCBT is predicated on these core foundational and functional competencies, it should be more likely to be accepted as being credible.

Evidence-Based Practice

Evidence-based practice includes the integration of "the best available research with clinical expertise in the context of patient characteristics, culture, and preferences" (APA Presidential Task Force on Evidence-Based Practice, 2006, p. 273). Randomised controlled trials (RCTs) or quasi-randomised controlled trials are required to suggest that a treatment is not only associated with but indeed causes positive outcomes. If the purpose is to establish the intervention's efficacy, then we are asking whether it works under controlled experimental conditions (i.e. experimental study design). The evidence would thus be obtained from analysing the results statistically. If the purpose is to establish its effectiveness in practice, then we are also focusing on obtaining statistical results from evaluation studies conducted in actual clinical settings (i.e. quasi-experimental).

CARE in the CHAIR Model

CARE in the CHAIR is a heuristic that I use to train my practicum students in developing a solid understanding of the therapeutic relationship and principles of change drawn from meta-analyses of RCTs that are common to all therapies. CARE represents congruence, alliance, regard, and empathy which are often referred to as the Rogerian principles but are not limited to person-centred therapy (Norcross & Goldfried, 2019). They are also core factors in demonstrating respect for the dignity of the client. Two other factors are also identified, which are alliance rupture-repair and supportive self-disclosure. Thus, we could extend this to CARERS, but managing ruptures and self-disclosures fall into the category of doing and thus are easier to examine when a specific case is reviewed.

CHAIR stands for corrective experience, hope, alliance, insight, and reality testing, which are considered to be some of the most important change principles across therapies (Eubanks & Goldfried, 2019). Corrective experiences provide opportunities for clients to challenge their old beliefs, develop healthier coping mechanisms, and experience more adaptive ways of interacting with the world. Hope emphasises the importance of instilling hope in clients and promoting positive expectations about their therapeutic journey. Hope from an Islāmic perspective has been explored in Rassool and Khan (2023) as an important construct to integrate into Islāmic psychotherapies. Perhaps, the strongest feature of hope from an Islāmic perspective is that it prevents despair.

I have had many instances where a client would be discussing their suicidal ideation with me and when I enquire into what prevents them from carrying it out, they reference their faith.

Client: If it weren't for my *deen* (my religion), I would have killed myself.
Mahdi: It sounds like your faith is literally saving your life.

The principle of increasing insight involves helping clients gain a deeper understanding and awareness of their thoughts, feelings, behaviours, and underlying issues. The working alliance refers to the collaborative and trusting relationship between the therapist and the client along with mutually agreeable goals and tasks to achieve those goals. Building a strong working alliance is foundational to successful therapy. A core aspect of CBT is the importance of evidence and from a transtheoretical perspective, ongoing reality testing is about encouraging clients to challenge their assumptions, perceptions, and beliefs in the context of their daily lives. It involves helping clients objectively evaluate their thoughts and actions to determine their accuracy and effectiveness. This process allows clients to make more informed and adaptive decisions and promotes the real-world application of therapeutic insights.

In Twomey, O'Reilly, and Goldfried (2023), their survey aimed to determine if there was consensus among a diverse group of psychotherapy clinicians and researchers regarding the presence of the five proposed transtheoretical principles of change. The participants, totalling 1,998 individuals, represented various theoretical orientations and completed an online survey.

The survey results demonstrated consensus which supports the importance of these principles in routine psychotherapy practice and aligns with previous research on their positive associations with therapy outcomes. Thus, further enhancing the significance of examining these principles in psychotherapy practice.

RCTs and CBT Manuals

But where does all this evidence on religiously modified CBT actually come from? To answer this question, we need to turn to how RCTs are constructed. An RCT is a research study design that is constructed to assess the effectiveness of an intervention or treatment. It's considered one of the most robust methods for evaluating the impact of treatments or interventions in scientific research (Trochim, n.d.). An RCT is constructed by randomly assigning participants to different groups, one of which receives the intervention being studied. The study is carefully designed to minimise bias, and the outcomes are compared between the groups to determine the intervention's effectiveness. The intervention itself needs to be structured, which is often done in the form of a manual to provide the facilitators or therapists with a structured guideline to follow to ensure that everyone received the same intervention. Deviation from the manual would be considered a potential error in the study. It is for this reason that criticisms against manualised treatments are made. However, in research, this is necessary to reduce bias and error, whereas in actual practice, deviating from the standard approach is not only expected but also preferred.

Beck, Rush, Shaw, and Emery's manual, *Cognitive Therapy of Depression* (Beck et al., 1979), not only outlined a detailed treatment protocol for cognitive therapy but also included research findings that demonstrated the effectiveness of this treatment approach. This research provided empirical evidence supporting the use of cognitive therapy as an effective treatment for depression. As a result, the manual not only provided clinicians with a structured approach to therapy but also solidified the scientific foundation of cognitive therapy, making it one of the most widely used and evidence-based forms of psychotherapy for various mental health conditions, including depression and anxiety.

Culture, Preferences, and Religion

When citing research, I chose to first utilise what is considered the highest form of evidence, namely meta-analyses of RCTs, to which there are plenty with respect to CBT and a sufficient degree of religiously adapted CBT. For Islām, it would be the Qur'ân and the Prophetic traditions known as the *aHadīth* (Rassool, 2021). For CBT, these principles and practices would be derived from the specialisation known as behavioural and cognitive psychology

(Klepac et al., 2012), whereas the flexibility component involves all of the factors related to adapting the approach to a specific client in therapy; three of these are emphasised and considered to have the highest level of empirical support: culture, preferences, and religion (Norcross & Wampold, 2018).

Norcross and Wampold systematically reviewed the literature on the impact of adapting treatment to the strength of the therapeutic alliance and therapeutic outcomes. They concluded that adapted approaches yield better outcomes than non-adapted versions of the same treatment, and adapting to the client's culture, preferences, and religion is heralded as having the highest effect sizes followed by adapting to the client's stage of change, coping styles, and reactance. That is, in a meta-analysis of 51 RCTs consisting of a total of 16,269 patients, treatments adapted to the client's therapy preferences compared to those that were not demonstrated an effect size of 0.28 on the quality of the therapeutic alliance. In culturally adapted treatments, 99 studies with 13,813 patients demonstrated an effect size of 0.50. For religious/spiritual adaptation, 97 RCTs with a total of 7,181 subjects had an effect size between 0.13 and 0.43. This indicates that clinicians who can establish cultural fit can expect better therapeutic alliances than those who do not.

At least 21 studies exist to support the utilisation of culturally adapted treatments which have been shown to be more effective than unadapted treatments with a modest effect size (d=0.32). However, in these studies, the cultural worldview of those receiving treatment was the only key element with no additional details (Benish, Quintana, & Wampold, 2011). Furthermore, identifying factors related to the culture and religion of the client and therapist are often neglected in studies on common factors. For example, across 295 studies and over 30,000 subjects, very few factors related to the client or therapist's identity were examined (Flückiger, Del Re, Wampold, & Horvath, 2018). Additionally, even amongst the studies examining religious adaptation, very few included Muslims.

Challenges in Adaptations

Despite the tremendous evidentiary support that has been developed on culturally adapted interventions, there still remains a need for "developing culturally responsive interventions" (Hall et al., 2016). If these newly developed interventions are able to demonstrate fidelity to the well-established research on change principles as well as fidelity to the core principles of the culture they are intended to be used for, it would be ideal. However, treatment fidelity is one common factor that may cause a challenge for practitioners aiming to adapt their approach to the client's transdiagnostic variables (Norcross et al., 2016). But it should be noted that unlike the importance of standardisation in research, modifications are often expected and necessary in practice. Especially since not every evidence-based treatment is applicable to all people or real-world settings. Thus, therapist expertise often comes with a strong sense of judgement on shifting the approach or modifying existing ones based on client factors (e.g. culture, preferences, characteristics) and progress outcomes. For IMCBT, expertise would also include Islāmic knowledge that can be enhanced through professional development. Thus, it should be noted that just as practitioners may lack certain competencies in the early part of their career, professional development is a fundamental aspect of all professions.

Lipstick on a Pig Is Still Haram (Forbidden) to Eat

Although adaptations are highly encouraged, they too need to be done in context since accommodation without any attention paid to the client's problem is not optimally effective (Yulish et al., 2017). Thus, balancing flexibility and fidelity is required (Chu & Leino, 2017), and knowing how and when to modify an intervention is key. Furthermore, the adaptations themselves may need to be done in a more rigorous fashion than what is currently available.

In their scoping review of the literature on Islām and psychology between 2006 and 2015, Haque et al. (2016) noted that Islāmic interventions are "perhaps the least-developed area in the current research" (p. 86). In critically appraising the content of the studies, the authors identified the need for deeper integration of Islāmic principles and concepts into treatment interventions and models. However, without a proper methodology to integrate Islām and psychology, the Islāmic worldview may be the one that gets deteriorated in the process of trying to have it become accepted or amenable to the scientific process. In Badri (2007), the author cautions those aiming to Islāmicise psychology not to engage in a process by which they are "unknowingly secularising Islām" (p. 1). He adds that painting a deteriorating house doesn't make it better structurally, rather, it represents the idea of a facade or an outward cover that tends to hide the structural imperfections. I like to add that putting lipstick on a pig still makes it haram (forbidden) to eat for Muslims and, thus, just adding Islām does not make an intervention evidence-based; attention needs to be paid to the systematic process required.

Religiously Modified CBT Manuals

Duke University's Centre for Spirituality, Theology and Health provides free access to Religiously Integrated Cognitive Behavioral Therapy (RCBT) manuals and workbooks for both the therapist and client. Each of the religiously adapted manuals addresses a specific faith. For Muslims, there is a Sunni and a Shi'a version. All of the manuals are based on an adaptation of Aaron Beck's original manual; for example, the conventional manual (Propst, Robins, Pearce, & Koenig, 2014) and the Christian manual (Ciarrocchi, Schechter, Pearce, & Koenig, 2014). The Sunni-Muslim version is a variant of the Christian manual. Each manual instructs the users to maintain a high degree of adherence to the manual. In the conventional manual, they add that "therapists are encouraged not to address religious or spiritual issues as part of the treatment" (p. 5). They explain that since it is quite likely that clients will bring these issues up, the therapist is instructed to "respectfully listen and then gently redirect patients to address the issues using a conventional CBT model" (p. 5).

However, it should be noted that the purpose of this manual was to conduct the RCT comparing the conventional approach to the religiously adapted approach thus making standardisation an essential feature. In particular, the information taught, the order in which it is taught, and the way it is taught should be similar across clients, despite the presenting concerns likely being different. Furthermore, clients are informed that the purpose is both treatment and research. Thus, the distinction between RCBT in research and practice should be considered, as flexibility is essential to evidence-based practice.

Dynamic Bilingualism

Another theme that runs throughout this book (and my practice) is referred to as *dynamic bilingualism* and is related to the flexibility principle. Dynamic bilingualism acknowledges the evolving, interconnected nature of bilingual practices emphasising the complexity of linguistic interactions and adaptations across contexts (García, 2009). This principle amalgamates multiple foundational competencies (Fouad et al., 2009) with several other promising applications. The clinical application of this theme (or behavioural anchor) can be seen in one's ability to explain the rationale for an intervention to be credible to a specific Muslim client from both scientific and Islāmic worldviews without compromising the fidelity to either. By doing so, one is able to claim that the intervention is indeed credible to both epistemic communities and meaningful to the client.

You Say Izlam, I Say Islām

The first indicator of credibility is acceptance or, simply, non-rejection. Often, language and cultural barriers have been implicated in reasons why many non-dominant groups (also referred to as minorities by some) including Muslims do not utilise psychological services (APA, 2021; Tanhan & Young, 2022). Although speaking two languages (English and Arabic) is one way to look at dynamic bilingualism, it goes far beyond alternating between the two or simply translating terms. Psychotherapy is also known as talk therapy as the primary tool often used is verbal and non-verbal communication, thus the importance of language use cannot be understated. Consider how the word Islām is pronounced and defined.

Linguistically, when an "s" follows a vowel, it is usually pronounced as a "z". This may be why most English-speaking people who do not speak any Eastern languages tend to pronounce Islām with a "z". But if that were the only reason, then why do we pronounce ISIS with an "s"? A linguist may say, well, because like iris, when the "s" comes after an unvoiced or quiet consonant, it is pronounced as an "s". Those specialising in discourse analysis may find certain concepts fascinating, whereas the rest of us may decide that this is such a minor issue that it is not worth spending any time on. I would be inclined to agree with the latter while also recognising that when others believe so strongly in something or identify wholly with a system, an attack on any part of that system can be taken personally.

Recently, the APA has released a document outlining eight major challenges and nine resolutions they aim to resolve with respect to healthcare in their effort to dismantle systemic racism against people of colour in the United States (APA, 2021). This testimony of the tension that already exists between White dominant and non-White non-dominant groups is further demonstrated in many other problems related to education, science, work, economic opportunities, criminal and juvenile justice, early childhood development, government, and public policy. Thus, therapists who hold negative views of Islām or biases against people of colour need to recognise how this will likely lead to struggles in truly respecting the dignity of those we serve, especially in being non-judgemental, empathetic, congruent, and holding the client in positive regard; all essential ethical and evidence-based practice principles from a psychology (Norcross & Goldfried, 2019) and Islāmic worldview.

Islāmic Psychology or Peace Psychology

In the development of Islāmic psychology, having a clear and concise definition of the concept of "Islāmic" is essential. From a linguistic standpoint, "Islām" is not originally an English word. However, when translated to English, it can mean "peace", but it can also be translated as "submission". However, we do not call it "Submission Psychology" or "Peace Psychology" just as "Cognitive Behavioural Therapy" isn't referred to as "Thought Action Therapy". While these terms can be used interchangeably, within their respective contexts, they hold specific meanings. Thus, defining what it means to be Islāmic requires some constructive clarity. According to Rassool (2021), to be Islāmic, all of the criteria must be met which means

> it must adhere to authentic sources and proofs that are employed to understand human nature and behaviour from an Islāmic perspective.
>
> (p. 19)

One common theme among all Islāmic scholars (including scholars in the field of Islāmic psychology) is their acceptance that to be Islāmic, it needs to be rooted in evidence derived from primary Islāmic sources, which are the Qur'ân, *aHadīth* (prophetic traditions), and scholarly consensus.

It is strongly encouraged to engage in deep personal reflection on verses from the Qur'ân. However, to conduct exegesis (*tafsir*), such interpretations and critical examinations require a high level of education and competence and is often carried out by scholars, theologians, and religious experts. Furthermore, anything the Prophet (ﷺ) did, said, or conferred upon is to be taken by Muslims as encouragement and depending on the context, possibly even obligatory. These traditions, also known as the *sunnah*, are found in compilations that have undergone a rigorous process of authentication. For example, Sahih Bukhârî is one of the most fundamental compilations of prophetic traditions and a resource not only for laypeople but also for scholars. Thus, like the Qur'ân, engaging in deep reflection is encouraged, but conducting analysis and exegesis (*tafsir*) requires expertise. Furthermore, to derive principles and rulings from it also requires a high level of education and training that could be part of one's professional development. Where to go to get such knowledge is beyond the scope of this book.

Although applied Islāmic and psychological sciences are two distinct fields with many facets and different views on what constitutes evidence, truth, knowledge, and other fundamental philosophical foundations (e.g. ontology, epistemology, praxis), scholars from both applied disciplines would agree that evidence-based practice is an essential requirement for credibility. Even if they do not agree on the nature of evidence itself (i.e. causality), they would agree on the purpose behind using evidence or the outcomes, which would be to enhance the health, well-being, and prosperity of people. What often remains a challenge is when and how best to do it in the context of psychotherapy; an area that the emerging discipline of Islāmic psychology is still grappling with. Thus, to reiterate, IMCBT is characterised as a culturally adapted and localised version of CBT prioritising the client's preferences, culture, and religion. Thus, it is built on a strong evidentiary basis while also maintaining fidelity to the core principles and processes of behavioural and cognitive psychology. The premise here is that any therapy that maintains fidelity to such fundamentals should be considered a credible application of CBT.

2 Conceptualising Islāmically Modified Cognitive Behavioural Therapy as a Convert Grandchild of Secular Parents

Kaplick and Skinner (2017) categorise Islāmic psychology under three approaches. The first one, deemed the filter approach championed by Dr Malik Badri, suggests utilising Islāmically compatible psychology approaches. The second one is referred to as Islāmic psychology. Psychology approach is an extension of the filter approach but also endorses focusing on developing uniquely Islāmic perspectives on human nature and the nature of problems. Furthermore, in this approach, the change process is derived from classical scholars and early Muslim philosophers, particularly from a Sufi paradigm. The third one is Hussain's comparative approach, which seeks equivalents of Western theories in Islāmic tradition instead of criticising them. Philosophically speaking, it would appear that the differences are whether to emphasise ontology (nature of being) or epistemology (nature and evaluation of knowledge) and how best to go about it. Agilkaya-Sahin (2019) argues that there is no clear-cut dissociation between these approaches, and they are likely to overlap. Seedat (2021) argues that the comparison approach aims to identify convergences between Islām and psychology while the filter approach is concerned with incorporating "indigenous" Islāmic psychological practices into contemporary psychology (p. 2).

Rassool (2021) further categorises the approaches as schools of thought, namely the orientalist approach, the integrationist approach, and the "Tawhîd Paradigm" approach. The orientalist approach is criticised for its lack of integration of Islāmic traditions and could be perceived as reinforcing colonisation (Seedat, 2021). The integrationist approach is similar to what was referred to as the Islāmic psychology approach with a focus on traditional scholars predominantly rooted in a Sufi-based school of thought. The *tawhîd* paradigm is an approach based specifically on the two essential bodies of knowledge for Muslims which are the Qur'ân and the *sunnah* (prophetic traditions) and tends to not endorse the Sufi paradigm. This approach, similar to the filter and comparison approach, retains the theory and practice of secular psychology that are considered to not be in violation of Islāmic beliefs and practices.

Metaphorically speaking, irrespective of which approach is taken, a common ground can be identified in the roots and the fruits, but the trunk and

DOI: 10.4324/9781003364207-3

branches (pathways and goals) will differ. However, I posit a possible fourth approach called the "convert approach". This approach can address the common critiques of each of the aforementioned and synthesise each stage sequentially. The convert approach consists of a filtration phase, a uniquely Islāmic phase, and a comparative phase that satisfies the need for fidelity to the evidentiary basis that any particular psychology specialisation is derived from while also being Islāmic. It is this approach that was used to develop IMCBT.

IMCBT: The Convert Grandchild of Behavioural and Cognitive Psychology Parents

IMCBT can be looked at as being a convert with secular grandparents. That is, if we assume that CBT is a child of behavioural and cognitive psychology. Thus, to say that IMCBT is just a child of CBT would not be fully accurate as it does not carry all of the DNA that makes up CBT (in particular some of its philosophical underpinnings related to evolutionary biology). But to say that it is not is also inaccurate since it certainly belongs to the family of cognitive behavioural psychology as it meets all of the necessary criteria and is thus fully compatible. Thus, rather than being a distant cousin, conceptualising IMCBT as a grandchild of behavioural and cognitive psychology parents who have converted to Islām is a more meaningful analogy.

That is, it retains its lineage but has chosen to adopt slightly different foundational beliefs. Furthermore, converting to Islām does not require changing all of one's cultural identity nor does it strip one away from their individuality. Ultimately, the individual's biology and personality remain the same, and thus certain modifications may be made, but essentially they are still the same person. That is, despite certain core differences related to beliefs (or philosophical assumptions), the convert is biologically and culturally still part of the family. Like its grandparent, IMCBT upholds the core principles of CBT such as the cognitive behavioural model, the change process characterised by learning theory, the importance of the therapeutic relationship, and a set of evidence-based interventions that are rooted in the biological, cognitive, and affective bases of behaviour. Likewise, in IMCBT, it is assumed that physical and mental health challenges are indicated by impairments in occupational and social domains. This is consistent with the DSM 5's conceptualisation of psychological disorders.

Like its grandparent, IMCBT adheres to a bio-psycho-social model but emphasises culture and religion. While spirituality is often subsumed under cultural factors in literature on CBT in IMBCT, it is emphasised as its own domain with varying degrees of relevance to other domains pending on the client. Additionally, whereas religion is often limited to coping strategies, IMCBT draws from the wealth of wisdom in Islam to facilitate problem solving and treatment planning. Furthermore, it infuses religion and spirituality throughout the therapeutic process through mild or deep modifications. For example, a mild adaptation may not require any deeper discussion on change mechanisms but could be a simple translation and comparison; like connecting the objectives of therapy to the objectives in Islām. For example, when we discuss the domains of health and well-being, we can align these with the objectives of Islāmic law at the individual level of analysis. Thus, the physical, psychological, social, and occupational domains are included while also ensuring that the spiritual domain is included based on the client's preferences. In turn, this can effectively address the psychological and spiritual needs of Muslim clients while achieving the objectives of both epistemic communities – Islām and psychology. Without the guiding principles, the perceived incompatibility between the two fields and the critiques against Islāmic integration with psychology would likely remain as strong factors in reducing the credibility of such an approach. Thus, turning to a discussion on compatibility and critiques is warranted.

CBT and Islām Share More Than "We Think"

Although the convert grandchild analogy has its utility in building bridges between scholars within and between the disciplines, it is not enough to comprehensively address many other challenges with credibility; especially ones that are based on logical fallacies (the enemy of philosophical thought and the source of many problems from a CBT perspective). The first is a fallacy with respect to comparisons, and the rest can be called Islāmically modified CBT critiques (although probably grammatically incorrect). The following can be used as recommended dialogue when explaining the rationale behind CBT to someone who may be doubting its compatibility.

Logical Fallacies Related to Compatibility

Often, the question of compatibility between Islām and psychology gets raised. It is important to clarify the fallacy in the question itself. That is, to label Islām and psychology as entirely incompatible or completely compatible would be committing a logical fallacy due to aspects that are incommensurable (they just don't mix and thus cannot be measured). Islām and Psychology have their own complexities and differences that make a direct overall comparison problematic. Instead of attempting such a broad comparison, it's more effective to break down their individual elements and gradually build a credible understanding by analysing them one at a time. Identifying the specialisation and core foundational competencies is a good place to start. However, the quality of the comparison needs to be evaluated. For example, to say that CBT and Islām are compatible because both focus on thoughts is too shallow to be meaningful. Thus, it's more than just "we think", as this would apply to almost everyone. Also, whatever conclusions are drawn should not be done just because "we think" so; rather, some form of systematic process to provide evidence of compatibility is needed.

Fidelity to the Islāmic Evidence

IMCBT maintains that evidence derived from Islāmic sources should undergo a rigorous and systematic process. One of the challenges of using a verse from the Qur'ân in an ad hoc fashion is that it can lose its context and be interpreted incorrectly (not to be conflated with personal reflections and contemplations (i.e. *taddabur*)). For example, in the example used in the RCBT manual (Sabki et al., 2018), the authors state:

> Even prophet Muhammad (ﷺ) is also encouraged in the Koran [Qur'ân] not to be so hard on himself: as God says to him, we have not sent down the Koran to you for you to be distressed (20:2); so we could be taught that being hard on ourselves can sometimes be dysfunctional.
>
> (p. 24)

According to reputable and widely agreed-upon scholarly Islāmic sources, this is not the proper interpretation of this verse. Rather, in *Tafsir Ibn Kathir* (Ibn Kathir, 2000), the context of the verse was in response to the disbelievers at the time who claimed that "this Qur'ân was only revealed to Muhammad to cause him distress". In Ibn Kathir, multiple explanations from a range of scholars affirm the point that "whomever Allāh gives knowledge to, it is because Allāh wants him [or her] to have an abundance of good". This is supported by the following Hadīth.

> To whomever Allāh wills goodness, He grants them understanding of the religion.
>
> (Bukhârî (a))

Although my only contention with this is that the Islāmic evidence used was likely not done with rigour (which was not a feature that needed to be part of their research), the intention and objective behind the intervention can still be sound despite better alternatives being available. If no rigorous systematic process is used, then in real practice, the theological reflection should come from the client or be phrased as a type of supportive and strategic self-disclosure. However, there are other more pressing challenges with similar styles of using the Qur'ân or Hadīth without fidelity to the Islāmic evidence.

Fidelity Without Flexibility

What is perhaps more problematic is when fidelity alone is used without flexibility. This can be seen when advice is given without any relevance to the client's context and serves to suppress or shame the person rather than progress and process. It may come off as toxic positivity or preachy proclamations. The evidence to support the negative impact of toxic positivity can be drawn from research on the physiological and cognitive impact of suppressing emotions. For example, higher levels of negative affect, lower levels of positive affect, poorer social adjustment, and decreased well-being have been linked to repeated suppression of emotions (Campbell-Sills, Barlow, Brown, & Hofmann, 2006).

Furthermore, whereas negative self-statements would be one part of the cognitive conceptualisation, it is important to not assume that positive self-statements are the only answer. With individuals who have low self-esteem, positive self-statements can have a negative effect (Wood et al., 2009). Thus, it is important to note that positive and pleasant thinking is not the objective in CBT but rather rational and evidence-based thinking. Text without context is one way of putting this, but I would prefer to elaborate on how I conceptualise the difference between counselling and advice.

Counselling Versus Advice

The way I often discuss the difference between advice and counselling is that advice is saying the right things, whereas counselling is responding to the right things. Although advice may be meaningful, adapting it to the client's context is much more meaningful and effective. In the context of therapy, fidelity and flexibility are all about adapting to the particulars of the client based on the generalities of the research (Norcross & Wampold, 2018). This would include, amongst many other things, sharing Islāmic knowledge that is relevant to the person and in the proper context. This can include a multitude of factors which will be explored throughout the book. However, the danger in the lack of attention paid to the context of the individual is that it can inadvertently cause spiritual harm to the client.

Ali ibn Abi Talib, may Allāh be pleased with him, said, "Speak to people only according to their level of knowledge. Would you like for Allāh and His Messenger to be denied?" (Bukhârî (b)).

Thus, the level of knowledge is one aspect that needs to be considered; however, it is also important to understand how the person may interpret what is being said based on their contextual factors. The danger could be a misunderstanding or misconception of what Allāh or his Messenger (PBUH) said which would lead to rejection based on faulty information.

Judgement and *Hikmah* (Wisdom)

While knowledge and skills are essential components of effective therapy, judgement plays a crucial role in determining when and how to apply those skills in a given therapeutic context. Judgement involves the capacity to make sound decisions based on a combination of knowledge, skills, clinical experience, and ethical considerations; also known as *hikmah* in Islāmic terminology derived from the following Qur'ânic verse.

- *Invite to the way of your Lord with wisdom and good instruction, and argue with them in a way that is best. Indeed, your Lord is most knowing of who has strayed from His way, and He is most knowing of who is [rightly] guided.*

(An-Nahl 16: 125, interpretation of the meaning)

The manual for RCBT for Muslims also references this verse but does not explain it. At first, one might assume that this is a criticism (which might be from an academic lens), but from an Islāmic perspective this is quite praiseworthy.

Zayd ibn Thabit reported: The Messenger of Allāh (ﷺ) said,

> May Allāh brighten the face of a person who hears a tradition from us and he memorises it until he can convey it to others. Perhaps he will convey it to one who understands better than him, and perhaps one who conveys knowledge does not understand it himself.
>
> (Abi Dawud (a))

Thus, *hikmah* in therapy could encompass the therapist's ability to assess and understand the unique needs and circumstances of each client and to tailor their interventions accordingly. It allows therapists to tailor interventions that are sensitive to clients' biological, psychological, and sociocultural factors, promoting more competent, effective, and culturally responsive therapy (Hays, 2016; Sue & Sue, 2019). However, in cases where you may not understand the Hadīth or verse from the Qur'ân, you can simply state it to the client and ask them for how they understand it. This would allow the therapist to remain cautious not to interpret Islāmic sources without the proper credentials while also encouraging *taddabur* or deep reflection by the client.

Critical Appraisal of Research on Using the Qur'ân in Therapy

Understanding and evaluating the evidence supporting cognitive behavioural psychology (Klepac et al., 2012) is an important knowledge and skill requirement to possess. For instance, consider a recent meta-analysis on the effects of prayer. It's important to note that while the findings from such studies may hold valuable insights, there are potential pitfalls that can be misleading. Some of the studies might lack methodological rigour, and the presence of confounding variables can cloud the interpretation of results. However, for practitioners, what truly matters is the practical benefit observed among the participants in these studies rather than the pursuit of broad generalisations as researchers might aim for.

In Owens, Rassool, Bernstein, Latif, and Aboul-Enein's study (2023), the authors conducted a scoping review with a focus on studies that use Islāmic sources as the primary or additional health intervention. Among 1,625 articles, 44 met the criteria and were analysed and indicated that various Qur'ânic practices, including praying, listening to recitations, and supplications, could effectively reduce stress, anxiety, and depression while enhancing coping strategies. However, as is often the case with most studies of this nature, the underlying mechanisms on why this appeared to work are missing. Nonetheless, they conclude that cultural accommodation and recognising social support within the Muslim community should be emphasised, as this could be one reason why such interventions provided the outcomes they did; a point that Bowland, Edmond, and Fallot (2012) also identify in their religiously modified CBT for Christians.

Owens, Rassool, Bernstein, Latif, and Aboul-Enein (2023) further caution that researchers should avoid essentialising Islām and focus on culturally responsive approaches to better understand the relationship between religion, culture, and mental health in Muslim populations and that further research is needed to explore and tailor interventions accordingly. Furthermore, the researchers identified key themes and sub-themes in the reviewed studies. One major theme that continues to be repeated with respect to recommendations is mainly on strengthening the rigour and methodology of the studies or focusing on other evidence-based interventions related to present-moment awareness (mindfulness) and social support. However, this is more of a general recommendation that can be important in practice.

Third-Variable Problem

Rather, with respect to the methodological issues, examining the third-variable problem is essential (simply put, something else that may better explain the positive effect). That is, it was unclear what the context was when the Qur'ân was listened to before sleeping, and if so, did it assist in sleep improvement? Such a critical appraisal would suggest that sleep is the mediating factor for anxiety and depression. That is, if we dig a little deeper, we can see that the interventions require further critical analysis if scientific rigour is to be applied. For example, the study by Zulkifli, Zain, Hadi, Ismail, and Aziz (2022) found that listening to nature sounds had a similar effect on reducing anxiety as listening to Qur'ânic recitation. The researchers attributed this similarity in outcomes to the fact that the participants' main language was not Arabic, and they may have had difficulty comprehending the verses used in the Qur'ânic recitation. Although this may suggest that language and comprehension may play a role in the effectiveness of Qur'ânic interventions for reducing anxiety in individuals from different linguistic backgrounds, they do not elaborate on why understanding the Qur'ân may enhance its effectiveness. Furthermore, the activating mechanism in listening to the Qur'ân could be interpreted as white noise, which could be an offensive way to use the Qur'ân with clients.

In the study conducted by Al-Jubouri, Isam, Hussein, and Machuca-Contreras (2021), it was observed that listening to music had a similar effect as listening to the Qur'ân in reducing anxiety levels in individuals prior to undergoing chemotherapy. Taken together, perhaps what the Qur'ân was being used for resembles white noise, which would not be what each study was targeting. Despite the diverse views in the literature, the use of the Qur'ân to support mental health is under-researched and under-theorised. The authors state that "Gaps appeared in the creativity and applicability of interventions for Muslim lifestyles and this may be one area offering the greatest gains" (p. 855). I wholeheartedly agree!

In sum, the multiple ways of adapting to a client can be looked at as both a science and an art as is commonly mentioned in the field. Certainly, there is no one specific way of doing it, and we may never know exactly what to do, but we approximate to the best of our abilities in a decision-making process guided by a sound systematic process. Similarly, in Islām, we may never know precisely what a Hadīth or verse truly means, but we utilise a systematic methodology to arrive at the best possible understanding. The operative word is "systematic" which should also be linked to a coherent theory that helps to explain the problem and change mechanisms.

3 Managing Stigma and the Case of Mr Shakib

For many, the prospect of therapy can be anxiety-inducing, regardless of societal stigmas. Not knowing what to expect is one challenge; however, in many cases, I also find that when the client has a misunderstanding of mental illness, it is important to address this early on. In therapy, understanding and addressing stigma requires a delicate balance of cultural sensitivity and evidence-based practices. Recognising cultural nuances and aligning therapy with religious beliefs help clients navigate stigma, cope with uncertainty, and address anxiety.

The case of Mr Shakib highlights the importance of navigating these concepts to create an effective therapeutic alliance and achieve meaningful change. Integrating Islāmic principles with evidence-based psychological techniques can lead to a more holistic and effective therapeutic approach; however, establishing a strong working alliance is essential, and using judgement on when to validate versus challenge is crucial.

The Case of Mr Shakib

The following case example will provide a demonstration of how working with Mr Shakib went beyond challenging irrational thoughts and focusing on deeper Islāmic principles. Furthermore, with highly religious clients, assessing for suicidal ideation needs to be done in a sensitive and creative manner, and it is more judicious to be done only after a strong therapeutic alliance has been formed.

Overview of the Presenting Problem

Mr Shakib was involved in a motor vehicle accident, which resulted in him being knocked unconscious. Since the accident, he has been experiencing physical pain and severe anxiety while driving. This has prevented him from returning to work as a driver in the transportation industry. He initially had strong concerns about seeking treatment due to the stigma associated with mental health challenges. Prior to the accident, Mr Shakib did not have any major physical complaints or psychiatric issues that required treatment or medication. He was generally healthy and despite some

DOI: 10.4324/9781003364207-4

common stressors had been managing quite well. However, the accident has had a significant impact on his psychological well-being and functioning. His strong belief that seeking psychological help is haram (forbidden) initially created a significant barrier making it challenging for him to receive support and serving as a precipitating factor. However, as his mental health continued to deteriorate, his physician strongly encouraged visiting a psychologist and despite his resistance, agreed due to knowing that the therapist (myself) was Muslim and would integrate Islāmic principles if he chose it.

Initial Intake

After a warm greeting and welcome to the office by the receptionist, the client, Mr Shakib, was offered tea, coffee, and snacks and escorted towards my office. Shortly into the session, after I asked him about his last experience while driving, he explained how scared he was since the accident and then in a lowered tone reluctantly said:

Shakib: But isn't mental health haram (Islāmically forbidden)?
Mahdi: What is mental health to you?
Shakib: You know, like *Majnoon* (Arabic word for insane).
Mahdi: Ahh, I see, earlier you said you were generally healthy, so which was it, healthy or sick?
Shakib: Ahh (a sign of approval).

Although the statement itself is not accurate, I was aware of what he was saying so I shifted to gaining a deeper understanding of his interpretation. The CBT intervention used here was challenging the cognitive distortion known as dichotomous thinking, also known as black-and-white thinking or all-or-nothing thinking. By introducing that a spectrum exists between health and illness, he immediately agreed with the point which allowed for a deeper explanation of mental health as a person's emotional, psychological, and social well-being encompassing how we think, feel, and behave. Furthermore, how it affects his ability to cope with everyday life stressors, maintain relationships, and make decisions made sense to him. Additionally, overcoming the conflation of *majnoon* with mental illness is more of a cultural stigma which was not a difficult challenge to overcome as his concern was not related to social stigma but rather a general reluctance due to personal religious beliefs. That is, there was a deeper issue that he was apprehensive about, which required going beyond the cultural references and into the deeper Islāmic beliefs about mental health; in particular, in relation to misunderstandings about what depression is.

Mahdi: Now let's get back to the question of haram. What are you referring to that is haram?

Shakib: Like depression.

Mahdi: Do you mean like *Huzn* (sorrow), *gham* (worry), *ham* (stress), *ghayth* (anger)?

Shakib: . . . (puzzled but with an intrigued look on his face).

Mahdi: Or do you mean *ya's* (hopelessness).

Shakib: Yes (followed by him quoting the verse in Arabic) "O My servants who have transgressed against themselves, do not despair of the mercy of Allāh".

Commentary

One recommended strategy to address the stigma of depression is normalising it. However, in responding to reactance that is associated with religious beliefs, it is important to ensure that cognitive challenge is not offensive or violates the client's worldview. Usually, saying something like, it's OK to be depressed, referring to the high percentage of people who have depression could have been damaging to the relationship, as it would neglect the deeper faith-based principle he is struggling with. Furthermore, accepting the client's worldview and prioritising it does not negate the need to challenge misunderstandings, so long as the challenge is in line with the client's worldview.

Thus, instead of using depression as the central concept to focus on, I used concepts related to negative emotions derived from the Qur'ân. These terms represent different states of emotional distress that even Prophets experienced, all of which can be associated with mental distress without *ya's* or hopelessness. I continued:

Mahdi: If that is so, then how would we go about explaining Yaqoub (I quoted the verse in Arabic). He cried himself blind, it was not out of happiness. As you know, the Prophet Muhammad (ﷺ) also cried.

Shakib: Saheeh (that's correct).

Commentary

Although there was no reason to mention the Hadīth as he was familiar with it, I will put it here for reference.

> Anas bin Malik narrates that "We went with Allāh 's Messenger (ﷺ) to the blacksmith Abu Saif, and he was the husband of the wet-nurse of Ibrahim (the son of the Prophet). Allāh 's Messenger (ﷺ) took Ibrahim and kissed him and smelled him and later we entered Abu Saif's house and at that time Ibrahim was in his last breaths, and the eyes of Allāh 's Messenger (ﷺ) (ﷺ) started shedding tears. 'Abdur Rahman bin 'Auf said, "O Allāh 's Apostle, even you are weeping!" He said, "O Ibn 'Auf, this is mercy". Then he wept more and said, "The eyes are shedding tears and

the heart is grieved, and we will not say except what pleases our Lord, O Ibrahim ! Indeed we are grieved by your separation".

(Bukhârî (c))

Furthermore, in cognitive restructuring, I find the best outcome is when the client verbalises the accuracy of the point rather than acquiescing to what I am saying. That is, clients saying "that is right" rather than "you are right" can be one indication of internalising the belief. As we continued to discuss the concept, Mr Shakib acknowledged the concept of sadness as not being a sin which ended with me light-heartedly saying, "now, the next time you hear it (Depression is Haram), you'll likely say astaghfirullah" to which he laughed and agreed. After engaging in this process of cognitive restructuring of the Islāmic variety, it was possible to begin discussing expectations from therapy and developing treatment objectives. That is, by adapting to the client's reactance, considering both culture and religion, we were able to transition into explaining what the process of therapy may look like; also from an Islāmic lens.

Mahdi: Therapy is more akin to a *Fatwa* (religious ruling) than a *Hukm* (general law). Like a fatwa, it's just for you, so it needs to be tailored.

This led to providing the Islāmically modified rationale behind the approach to treating his anxiety. The statement I used was "the cure for ignorance is inquiry" referring to a lengthy Hadīth whereby the Prophet Muhammad (ﷺ) identified ignorance as a serious problem and enquiry as the solution (Abi Dawud (b)). This was followed by stating the verse about asking those who know if you do not know (Al-Anbiya' (The Prophets) 21:72) which although in the Qur'ân is about asking the people of the scripture, the general principle is to consult knowledgeable experts.

Commentary

By grounding the rationale in Islāmic principles, it was easier to begin to explain the scientific theories I drew upon to conceptualise his anxiety. What also facilitates this process is reaffirming the centrality of the Islāmic perspective and providing a rational account of psychological theories as being one of many perspectives we can use.

Mahdi: Remember, psychology is just a lens, but mental health is part of the human experience. Also, we had counselling before English was even a language.

At this point, it was safe to continue to discuss evidence-based CBT interventions without any cultural and religious misunderstandings posing as a barrier or the need to deeply modify the interventions. For example, I discussed exposure therapy as the first intervention to address his anxiety around driving using the behavioural conceptualisation of how phobias develop.

Treatment Planning

The major goals involved in treating the client's anxiety involve working with the client to increase their understanding of their anxious feelings as well as to examine and challenge their irrational thoughts that may be contributing to the maintenance and/or aggravation of their symptoms. The treatment plan will also include helping the client improve their coping strategies and reduce their vulnerability. The client has also been experiencing various symptoms that cluster around a depressive disorder that require treatment. The goals we intend to work on include helping the client identify and better understand the factors that are maintaining their depressive mood. These would include their change in lifestyle since the accident as well as cognitive distortions and issues related to dependency, helplessness, and hopelessness. Both the depression and anxiety-related symptoms will be targeted in parallel.

Exposure-based therapies consist of various behavioural approaches that tend to focus on exposing the client to the object that causes fear. In this case, fear is related to driving. The conceptualisation of this case from a behavioural perspective suggests that the distress is maintained due to the avoidance. That is, by avoiding the stimuli, the client does not engage in the opportunity to learn that the fear can be tolerated, that it will reduce in intensity on its own rather than by engaging in escape or avoidance behaviours, and that the perception of fear and the associated catastrophe will not come true nor will it be as bad as they expect.

Avoidance can be of two kinds: not engaging at all or not engaging fully. Through exposure therapies, the treatment is designed such that the client can experience the fear-inducing stimulus directly (also known as in-vivo exposure) or through imagination (also referred to as imaginary exposure). As the fear hierarchy is developed, starting from low or mild anxiety-provoking contexts and then gradually into the most severe or highest fear-inducing context, the client couples relaxation strategies with exposure to the stimulus, and the process of weakening the association between fear and the context begins.

Systematic desensitisation is one type of exposure therapy that can be done without direct exposure and in a safe way. It also includes a fear hierarchy coupled with relaxation strategies (or other responses incompatible with fear). This has the intended outcome of weakening the fear associated with the stimuli (in this case driving). Although in vivo exposure tends to be better for quicker outcomes, systematic desensitisation can be more effective for changing rather than reducing avoidance. In this case, the client will be guided on how to utilise both in their goal of returning to pre-accident levels of confidence in driving and normal levels of anxiety while on the road.

Suicidal Ideation

As Mr Shakib was getting more comfortable opening up, he shared what he felt was deeply disturbing and very difficult to speak about. He had explained in his own way that he had thoughts that he would rather be dead which would be considered a mild form of suicidal ideation as he had no plans nor did he intend to harm himself, but in his mind, it is the most heinous of thoughts. Here, normalising this thought was done strategically but after establishing a strong bond of trust and respect as well as the feeling of cultural or religious safety (i.e. that his religious worldview was not going to be challenged or dismissed). I explained to him that most people I see experience these thoughts, and it is quite common in society, but it can also range on a spectrum of severity. I would add that thoughts that we would rather be dead tend to occur when we feel we don't have any other solution so we think about this as a dysfunctional solution. I will admit, in retrospect, I should have probably continued to validate his distress and shift to an emotion-focused coping stance, but this did not cause any ruptures. Rather, it is here where I understood how strong his religious coping was as without any probing, he identified the meaning of his pain for himself. He then stated a powerful coping strategy that confirmed for me that it is essential to continue to work with Mr Shakib using more deep Islāmic integration and CBT without the concern for spiritual shaming or preachy proclamations.

Shakib: I think it happened (referring to his thoughts of suicide) so I can make more *dhikr* (remembrance of Allāh).

Mahdi: You know, when you say that, I think it is so amazing. How you can shift from negative to positive like that (transitioning to Arabic). Only for the believer eh!

Shakib: (with a joyful expression on his face) *Alhamdulillah* [Praise to Allāh].

Commentary

The last statement is referencing a known authentic Hadīth which states

> Wondrous is the affair of the believer for there is good for him in every matter and this is not the case with anyone except the believer. If he is happy, then he thanks Allāh and thus there is good for him, and if he is harmed, then he shows patience and thus there is good for him.
>
> (Muslim (b))

Usually, shifting directly from negative to positive can be a type of invalidation or toxic positivity if no neutral transition is present. But in this case, when it comes from the client themselves, it is important to reinforce and praise this practice. By the end of the first session, it was clear that the working alliance was strong, and Mr Shakib has agreed to work together to identify and explore the different ways that the accident may have caused an alteration in their thoughts and beliefs. These changes are likely to affect both emotions and behaviours.

Session 2: Stigma of Medication

In the following week, although the client's anxiety around driving had been only slightly reducing, he was quite optimistic about continuing therapy and had explained that he had visited his physician and explained how pleased he was with the referral. He explained that his physician had recommended medication to manage his anxiety, to which Mr Shakib was quite reluctant once again. He took the prescription and instead of challenging the physician, he decided to bring it up with me first. In our session, after checking in on his mood and activities the previous week as well as conducting a brief assessment of his anxiety around driving, he asked me about taking medication, and my response was simply, "the best evidence we have for treating anxiety is when both psychotherapy and medication are combined" and reaffirmed the Islāmic position on the use of medication. This seemed enough for him to be confident in taking the medication, as he would report in a follow-up session that he has been feeling better after taking the medication.

Commentary

It's possible that the principle of asking questions and seeking advice from experts on things he wasn't sure about helped him think more logically about his views on medication. This approach could have encouraged him to gather information, consider different perspectives, and make a more informed decision based on evidence and knowledge from reliable sources. This way, he could have approached the topic of medication with a more balanced and rational mindset. Thus, the benefits of utilising IMCBT extend beyond the session and are likely to affect the use of logical thinking in other areas of the client's life. Addressing cultural and religious stigma associated with mental health requires normalising emotions, understanding cultural beliefs, and integrating religious teachings to counteract negative perceptions which can greatly facilitate rapport and trust. Fostering trust by demonstrating cultural competence and acknowledging the validity of the client's religious perspectives is critical. In this case, highlighting principles like seeking knowledge, expert advice, and embracing hope from Islāmic teachings aligns with therapeutic goals.

Building rapport, addressing religious concerns, and introducing the concept of mental health as a spectrum rather than binary categories allowed us to disentangle cultural stigma from genuine mental health concerns by using Islāmic principles that acknowledge the range of emotional distress found in the Qur'ân and experienced by the Prophets. This can be accentuated by accepting the client's worldview while gently challenging misunderstandings. Finally, recognising the client's coping strategies rooted in religious practices and principles as an outcome of other factors rather than as an intervention, to begin with, shows great promise. That is, by applying CBT techniques, therapists can challenge dichotomous thinking, normalise emotional experiences, and guide clients towards reframing negative emotions as opportunities for personal growth instead of providing advice and preachy proclamations.

4 Addressing Common Critiques of CBT and Islām

Explaining how the same misconceptions and criticisms against CBT are also made against Islām can provide a healthy common ground to build from (albeit one born in a shared problem with a similar solution; more evidence-based thinking). These so-called Islāmically modified CBT critiques are intended not only to provide a brief overview of common critiques of CBT but also to engage the reader in some critical thinking. Thus, I chose not to repeat what can easily be found in the extant literature but to provide a new perspective on old problems. For example, Tanhan and Young (2022) already provide a systematic review of the literature on Muslim mental health between 2002 and 2020. This review highlights the need for more research to be done in this area given that Muslims tend to be disproportionately underserved, under-researched, and misunderstood.

Furthermore, barriers to accessing services are often influenced by stigma, cultural beliefs, and a general misunderstanding and lack of knowledge about psychotherapy, further promoting the need for more culturally responsive services. Additionally, theoretical frameworks to utilise to gain a deeper understanding of Muslims are scanty, which is likely another factor as to why research that includes Muslims tends to lack implications for specialised practice and focuses more on general principles. Community awareness is often one of the most important activities to reduce the lack of awareness and misunderstandings. But the approach will need to be tailored to each specific community, beginning with a common misconception on the relationship between mental health challenges and *iman* (faith).

High *Iman* (Faith) Is All You Need

Rather than spending time trying to restructure the way Muslims think about psychology, it may be more meaningful to provide how the individual can personally benefit and allow them to see the wisdom (*hikmah*) in what you are saying, which may often be simpler than we think. I recall over eight years ago when I first began to approach community leaders to engage in mental health training, my first (arguably semi-successful) approach was to target

DOI: 10.4324/9781003364207-5

the needs of the imams (religious clergy). The conversation with the well-respected senior imam went something like this:

Mahdi: Imam, how long do your marriage counselling sessions usually last?
Imam: [a dreadful ufff followed by] sometimes three hours!
Mahdi: It must be very exhausting for you.
Imam: [Looks me straight in the eyes and says nothing but has a grimace on his face and I am aware he felt validated.]
Mahdi: What if I were to tell you that you can achieve the same outcome in 15 minutes?
Imam: [Wide-eyed but perhaps in disbelief] This would be excellent.

I proceeded to explain that we can develop a model to use based on his experience as well as using some evidence-based practices from psychology. Although at the time this did not lead to any progress, the seed was likely planted. Although he would refer clients to me, it was not until recently when I returned back to the city for a visit that I inferred that a transformation had certainly occurred (I had moved to another city and returned for a visit). After one of the noon prayers, the senior imam had gotten up and clearly stated to the audience the need for mental health services and emphasised my role in the community as bridging between Islām and psychology and asked me to give a few impromptu words. Thus, I capitalised on the moment with a script. I began by asking:

> Who believes that if we have high levels of *iman* (faith), we do not need to see a psychologist?

About half of the room of 100 people raised their hands. Perhaps, some of the other half may have been too shy or felt it would be disrespectful to disagree. Nonetheless, I too raised my hand and said

> You are right, if we had the highest level of *Iman*, we would not need Psychologists, prisons, police, or dentists, but since we do not have such a high level, we need health professionals to help us achieve that goal.

I went on to explain that from both a scientific and Islāmic perspective, both agree that mental health challenges impede our health, well-being, and healing. The shared goal is perhaps the only factor that truly matters with respect to our individual responsibilities towards our specific clients. However, the issues are not just negative views from founders in the field on religion but rather a general misunderstanding and misconceptions as Tanhan and Young (2022) note.

Mass Media and Macro-Level Issues

I recall a pleasant experience meeting a bright aspiring psychologist who was completing her degree in psychology and wanted to enhance her practical experience by working at my practice. During her interview, I had asked her about what branch of psychology she was hoping to pursue. She enthusiastically said, "forensic Psychology". I was amazed and asked, so you must really love statistics. She responded, "actually no I don't". I knew what was going on, so I probed deeper, and it was clear that her perception of forensics was probably what is often found in movies and crime shows that resemble the work from the behavioural sciences unit. The misunderstanding is in no way a challenge to her intelligence, it just demonstrates how powerful the media can be in forming our opinions, even the most intelligent of us. Likewise, it is important to recognise that misunderstandings around the field of psychology and Islām are often facilitated by popular culture. In movies, we tend to usually see a patient lying down on the couch speaking about their childhood, and hence the image of psychoanalysis permeates the view of psychology. The mental health therapist also ends up more often than not being the villain. The views of Muslims in the media are perhaps one of the most often discussed issues when speaking about systematic discrimination, also, playing the role of villain in every news story.

Simple, Not Simplistic

One oft-repeated critique of CBT is that it is too simple and focuses only on thoughts (Neenan & Dryden, 2020). Here, differentiating between simple and simplistic is key to a deeper understanding of this critique. It is simple in that the underlying principles and practices are easy to comprehend and learn; however, it is not simplistic in the sense that it is defined by focusing on thoughts. That is, while therapeutic techniques play a crucial role in the practice of a specific therapy, they do not solely define it. Rather, what truly characterises a therapy are its core features, which encompass the underlying principles, theoretical framework, and overall approach to case conceptualisation. In the case of CBT, it is essential to recognise that its essence is not limited to specific techniques like thought records. These techniques are akin to tools used in the construction of a factory, but they do not define the factory. The heart of CBT lies in its cognitive model (Beck, 2021), which forms the foundation upon which the therapy is built, and thus, just as a blueprint outlines the design of a factory, the cognitive model guides the approach and strategies used in CBT.

Similarly, understanding the tenets of Islām is simple, but they are not simplistic. Islām is a comprehensive way of life for its adherents, and the five pillars of Islām and six pillars of faith can comprehensively explain most of it. However, calling a therapy Islāmic simply because it translates a secular concept into an Islāmic term (e.g. like calling the belief in God a coping strategy) is not only offensive but also a distorted view of what it really is. Rather, it is the creed or core belief that defines Islām, which begins and ends with the sincerely held belief that none is worthy of worship except Allāh alone. It is this core belief that activates all other mechanisms that make a model truly Islāmic. Thus, to reiterate what Rassool (2021) states, to be Islāmic, it needs to adhere to all of the criteria as all of the criteria are interconnected as a blueprint.

Only Symptom Relief

Due to its brief nature and focus on the here and now, CBT has been accused of being simply a therapy for symptom relief (Neenan & Dryden, 2020). If symptom relief is the objective of therapy, then there is no problem accepting this as is. However, addressing the source of the symptoms can lead to lasting change. It should be noted that at times, making a conceptualisation of a person's problem too complex can be problematic. That is, being overly eager can be counterproductive as some may engage in deeper schema-focused therapy for uncomplicated issues (James, 2001). The presenting concern may not be rooted in the core beliefs or schemas but rather in a difficult situation that the person has been having negative, dysfunctional thoughts about.

Likewise, scholars who tend to reject the existence of God make a similar argument against people who believe in a higher power. Often, religion is explained in a type of symptomatic relief argument, such as existential writings of Yalom that "we create Gods for our comfort" (Yalom, 2002, p. 308). Freud, the founder of psychoanalysis, famously referred to religion as an "illusion" that provides comfort and security, akin to a child's relationship with their parents. Freud suggested that the concept of God and religious beliefs might arise from a psychological need for protection and control over the uncertainties of life. Although the core beliefs on human nature and change mechanisms in psychoanalysis would be easily rejected by those adhering to the tenets of behavioural and cognitive psychology, the views of Albert Ellis would not.

Too Rigid

Being too rigid and manualised is one of the more prominent critiques of CBT (Neenan & Dryden, 2020). After reading nearly every article I can get my hands on related to Islām and CBT, I realised that often, authors tend to criticise aspects of CBT that may have more to do with the difference between research and practice. In research, standardisation is necessary and valued, whereas in actual practice, flexibility is essential. One of the tenets of a good CBT is that it is culturally adapted and tailored to the specific context of the client (Beck, 2021).

But the same "rigidity" argument is levied against religion as well by proponents of CBT such as Albert Ellis, who claimed that devout religious belief mediates psychopathology (Ellis, 1980). From an academic perspective, it is important to acknowledge that Albert Ellis, a prominent figure in the field, indeed had personal views on religion that were critical and negative. As a scholar and therapist, Ellis was known for his strong beliefs in rationality and his promotion of secular humanism, which often led him to criticise religious beliefs and practices. Ellis saw religion as a potential source of dogma, guilt, and emotional disturbance, which he viewed as contrary to the principles of rational thinking and emotional well-being. Although it is possible to have irrational thoughts stemming from religious views, to label religion entirely irrational is neither ethical nor scientific. What matters most, however, is that therapeutic efficacy depends on the client's perception and comfort with the approach. If a client feels uncomfortable with a particular therapeutic method due to its historical associations or its potential conflict with their beliefs, it may be more beneficial to explore alternative approaches if you are unable to convince them otherwise; else refer them elsewhere.

Overgeneralisations

Despite Ellis's views on religion, to group all religions together as though they are a monolith is a fallacy. Although Islām shares many commonalities with Judaism, Christianity, Buddhism, Sikhism, and all other religions, it is in the core beliefs where high levels of incommensurability can be found. What is likely shared is more relevant to psychotherapy than theological beliefs, that is, ethical conduct and respect for the dignity of persons. Perhaps, the Islāmic principle of loving for your fellow brethren in humanity what we love for ourselves (also known as the Golden principle found in all faiths) is what should be focused on. Moreover, emphasising the potential strengths derived from the client's faith rather than any debates on the personal views of founders of the field would be in line with CBT (Beck, 2021). This is one benefit of engaging in the development of an integrated approach by analysing components rather than the whole. That is, founders of an approach, theories on human nature, and specific theories addressing specific issues are components that can each be examined for their degree of credibility.

Enhance Construct Clarity

In addition, construct clarity can help to maintain relationships despite beliefs that simply cannot mix (i.e. incommensurability). That is, where clashes are likely to arise may have more to do with a misunderstanding of the concept of secular than actual incompatibility. In Cucchi's (2022) narrative review, the author outlines the challenges associated with utilising CBT with Muslims with the term "secular" being the centrepiece of the debate. Defining secular and knowing that there are different types allows for communication to be enhanced. For example, if secularism is conflated with atheism, then dialogue between the scientific community and any other group that believes in God can be stunted due to terminological challenges rather than actual disagreements. If so, then these conflicts can be resolved through improved communication methods beginning with construct clarity. A more operational definition of secular may have more to do with what is focused on in terms of the nature of knowledge (epistemology) rather than matters of theology. Furthermore, the challenges highlighted in the APA's (2021) apology for systemic racism against people of colour perpetuated by the field will require a great deal of effort if healing and progress are to be achieved. Thus, having a systematic method of communication that increases acceptance between unnecessarily clashing parties may be appreciated by practitioners and policymakers alike; a method that should include a construct clarity process. Otherwise, they may continue to clash due to communication barriers rather than actual epistemological differences.

Be Sceptical About Scepticism

Perhaps, a more challenging issue to address has more to do with the philosophical underpinnings of the field related to research and education more so than what is found in real-world applications. For example, it is common for first-year psychology students to hear the phrase "Be sceptical" early in the semester when learning about research methods and other aspects related to developing competence in scientific mindedness. However, the concept of scepticism may indirectly alienate and marginalise non-dominant populations who may have interpreted the statement to be an attack on their personally held beliefs. I have had countless students ask me "is it haram" or forbidden to study psychology partially due to this (but perhaps mostly due to some of the assumptions around evolutionary biology or Freudian psychoanalysis).

Faith-based students may particularly struggle with rectifying their beliefs in the unseen with the principles of the scientific method, possibly leading some to abandon an academic trajectory in the field of psychology in exchange for something less controversial in their minds. During a time when the need for psychologists to represent diverse communities is both practical and critical, those teaching psychology would benefit from a deeper understanding of the implications of the concept of scepticism on their students. Additionally, students who are worried about what scepticism may mean for their religiously held beliefs can learn how scepticism as a form of critical thinking can lead to higher levels of faith in their belief. This is perhaps where IMCBT can be quite promising.

Part II

Theoretical Framework

5 Islāmically Modified Cognitive Behavioural Therapy Core Competencies

Traditional Ways of Being, Contemporary Ways of Doing

Fidelity involves utilising CBT in a consistent and faithful manner, ensuring that the core functional and foundational aspects of the therapy are implemented effectively and accurately. By maintaining fidelity, therapists uphold the integrity and effectiveness of CBT as a treatment approach. Recall, flexibility refers to the therapist's ability to adapt the treatment approach to meet the specific needs and characteristics of each individual client (i.e. clinical application). While fidelity to the core principles of CBT is important, it is also recognised that certain modifications may be necessary or beneficial to optimise therapy outcomes. By breaking down CBT into its component parts, we can better apply and evaluate each modification. In this chapter, the core knowledge requirements will be put forth followed by the Islāmic correlate.

Islāmic Correlates

The concept of Islāmic correlates here emphasises the intersection of psychological theories and interventions with Islāmic principles and values. In the context of psychological interventions, adapting approaches to align with the client's culture, religion, and preferences holds great value. Tailoring therapeutic techniques to incorporate elements of a client's faith and belief system can enhance the effectiveness of interventions and foster a stronger therapeutic alliance (Eubanks & Godfried, 2019). Moreover, just as connecting psychological models and interventions to biological correlates enhances the credibility of CBT within the broader health service field, integrating these theories with Islāmic correlates can enhance credibility among Islāmic scholars and Muslim clients.

CBT Core Knowledge Requirements

The core knowledge base for practice are the following (Klepac et al., 2012):

- An overview of the history of CBP
- The cognitive behavioural model and information processing model

DOI: 10.4324/9781003364207-7

- Biological/neurological correlates
- The relationship between learning theory and clinical change
- Basic understanding of the interactions between affect, behaviour, and cognitions (e.g. the bio-psycho-social model)
- Understanding and evaluating the evidence supporting cognitive behavioural model
- The philosophy of science and empirical research on the therapeutic relationship (discussed in other chapters)

Brief History

Psychology as an academic discipline has been developing, advancing, and applying psychological science since the late 1800s. The "wave" analogy is fitting to explain how research that leads to the development and advancement of theories and evidence-based practices progresses over time. The wave metaphor may lead some to assume that new waves wash away old ones, but this is certainly not the case. With each new wave, features of the previous waves are integrated into the new wave as they continuously transform the shore in new ways. What we see as the discipline of psychology today has undergone multiple transformations or waves with more likely to come.

The first two waves of cognitive behavioural therapy (CBT) mark significant developments in the field of psychotherapy. The first wave focused on behaviourism, emphasising observable behaviours and their modification through conditioning and reinforcement stemming back to Watson and Skinner (Watson & Rayner, 1920). The second wave integrated cognitive processes, acknowledging the role of thoughts and beliefs in shaping behaviour and emotions (Beck, 1967). This laid the foundation for the cognitive restructuring techniques that are central to modern CBT.

In the third wave of CBT, essential features of previous generations remain intact while growing to incorporate and synthesise "questions, issues, and domains previously addressed primarily by other traditions" (Hayes, 2004, p. 658). What seems essential in this process is that any modifications or integrations are evaluated "from a scientific point of view, with an interest in coherent theory, carefully assessed processes of change, and solid empirical outcomes" (p. 660). By doing so, the commitment to scientific empiricism remains paramount. The same should apply to Islāmic evidence, that Islāmic applications to CBT are also done in such a way that maintains fidelity to the scientific approach, which would be accomplished through a systematic process that identifies the theory, process of change, and outcomes.

Cognitive Behavioural Model

When first learning about CBT, often students are taught the famous quote by Epictetus (or a derivative of it) that "we are not disturbed by events but the interpretation of the events". This quote encapsulates the idea that our emotional reactions are not directly caused by events themselves but rather by how we perceive and interpret those events. The stoic philosopher Epictetus is often recognised as a key influence on CBT with pioneers such as Beck and Ellis acknowledging drawing from such ancient philosophical writings to shape their therapeutic methods. The alignment between the teachings of ancient philosophers and the current theoretical framework in CBT can be a powerful way to facilitate educating the client (or students) on the rationale for therapy and by extension, enhance acceptance.

Cognitive theory, as described by Beck and Dozois (2011), can be understood as a diathesis-stress model. In this model, the term "diathesis" refers to cognitive vulnerability, which encompasses maladaptive beliefs. On the other hand, "stress" pertains to ongoing adverse life events, which are the precipitating factors that trigger these maladaptive beliefs. The interplay between cognitive vulnerability and current adverse life events leads to the activation of these beliefs, forming the basis of cognitive theory. However, there are varying degrees of vulnerability, so a number of adverse life events may need to occur rather than just one before depression descends (Scott, 2009).

Information Processing Model

The information processing theory compares the human mind to a computer, highlighting processes such as attention, memory, and problem-solving. Beck's cognitive therapy (CT) is grounded in an information processing model, where accessed information is rationally processed. Healthy and adaptive functioning is thus enhanced through more rational, flexible, and accurate ways of cognitively processing experiences. When terrible things happen to us, unhelpful thoughts and beliefs can inhibit our ability to cope constructively and thus further aggravate our emotional distress. In other words, the way we process external information influences how we feel and act. When we process information rationally and accurately, it is indicative of more healthy and adaptive functioning, whereas inaccurate, rigid, and distorted interpretations of events often run contrary to rational and evidence-based thinking that provides a realistic and balanced view of events (Weishaar, 1996). Thus, in CT, the underlying pathological mechanism is distorted thinking (Ledley, Marx, & Heimberg, 2010), and distorted thinking (also referred to as thinking errors, dysfunctional thinking, and maladaptive thinking) is usually a result of dysfunctional intermediary and core beliefs.

Automatic Thoughts, Intermediary, and Core Beliefs

The information processing model behind CT proposes that dysfunctional thinking can be conceptualised at three different levels. They are automatic thoughts, which flow from intermediate beliefs (or underlying assumptions and rules) and are rooted in core beliefs. Automatic thoughts can be adaptive or maladaptive, positive or negative. Automatic thoughts are seen as problematic when they are not based on any evidence and are irrational leading to unrealistic and inflexible interpretations of experiences. They are related to intermediary thoughts or assumptions and beliefs. Mediating between the automatic thoughts and core beliefs are assumptions and rules that guide a person's actions and establish certain standards for being and doing. When such assumptions are illogical, they can lead to maladaptive ways of thinking and prevent the individual from exposing the core belief that sits at the root of the maladaptive style of thinking. According to Beck, Emery, and Greenberg (1985), these assumptions and rules tend to cluster around three main themes: control, acceptance, and competence.

Islāmically Modified Cognitive Behavioural Model

When working with Muslims who prefer Islāmic integration, providing the rationale for IMCBT can enhance acceptance by connecting specific Islāmic teachings to the pathological and change mechanisms model that underpins the therapeutic approach. The Islāmic perspective of *husnul than*, or promoting positive assumptions and avoiding negative suspicions, resonates strongly with the fundamental principle of healthy functioning in CBT. It is derived from the Qur'ânic verse that states "O believers! Avoid many suspicions, ˹for˺ indeed, some suspicions are sinful" (Al-Hujurat (The Apartments) 49:12). The Hadīth from the Prophet (ﷺ) states, "To have good thoughts (or suspicions) is from well-conducted worship" (Abi Dawud (c)). This Islāmic teaching encourages individuals to hold positive and constructive thoughts about others, promoting a mindset of optimism, trust, and goodwill.

Additionally, the teachings of the Prophet (ﷺ) further underline the significance of avoiding negative assumptions. He advised, "Avoid suspicion, for suspicion is the gravest lie in talk" (Muslim (c)), highlighting the destructive nature of baseless suspicions in interpersonal relationships. This aligns with the CBT principle of challenging irrational thoughts that lead to distorted perceptions and negative emotions. Imam Ghazali referenced one of the early Muslim scholars as saying "If a friend among your friends errs, make seventy excuses for them. If your hearts are unable to do this, then know that the shortcoming is in your own selves" (Seekers Guidance, 2010).

Biological/Neurological Correlates

While biological correlates are significant in psychological research, it's important to acknowledge that they belong to distinct fields. This highlights the potential of interdisciplinary research where combining insights from different domains can yield a more comprehensive understanding of human behaviour and well-being. Connecting psychological interventions to biological or neurological correlates is considered important because it also helps provide a more comprehensive understanding of how these interventions work at a physiological level, enhancing the scientific foundation of psychological practices and theories. This integration contributes to the credibility and effectiveness of interventions by linking psychological changes to observable changes in the brain and body, most notably the work of Donald Hebb (1949).

Neurons Wire Together, If They Fire Together

The idea of neuroplasticity led to a major shift in the way we understand the brain and by extension, human behaviour. Neuroplasticity or neural plasticity is defined as "the ability of the nervous system to change in response to experience or environmental stimulation" ("Neuroplasticity," n.d.(a)). That is, the brain can undergo a process whereby it functions in a different way than it previously did. At the most basic level, the famous phrase, "neurons wire together, if they fire together" represents a model of learning that can underpin behaviourism. In learning theory, this Hebbian rule explains how memory is formed. This style of associative learning starts with an experience which then triggers neurons that form a neural network. When repeated, the brain then triggers the same neurons each time.

Learning Theory

Learning theory refers to a set of psychological theories that explain how individuals acquire new knowledge, skills, behaviours, and attitudes through experiences and interactions with their environment. These theories emphasise the role of environment, stimuli, and reinforcements in shaping human learning. Several prominent learning theories have been proposed by psychologists, each offering a unique perspective on the learning process. These include classical conditioning, operant conditioning, social learning theory, and cognitive learning theory – these can be found in any introductory textbook on psychology.

Classical conditioning (Pavlov, 1927) focuses on how associations are formed between stimuli and responses, whereas operant conditioning (Skinner, 1938) centres on the relationship between behaviour and its consequences. It suggests that behaviours followed by positive outcomes are likely to be repeated, whereas those followed by negative outcomes are less likely to be repeated. Social learning theory (Bandura, Ross, & Ross, 1961) emphasises the role of observational learning and modelling. It suggests that people learn by observing others' behaviours, attitudes, and outcomes. Cognitive learning theories, which include the information processing theory as well as notable theories like cognitive-developmental theory (Piaget, 1952), focus on internal mental processes and how they contribute to learning. Piaget's theory emphasises the stages of cognitive development that individuals pass through as they acquire new knowledge. These learning theories offer insights into how individuals acquire knowledge and skills, and they continue to influence educational practices, behaviour modification techniques, and our understanding of human development.

Process of Change or Change Mechanisms

Change in CBT is commonly related to changes in core beliefs and schemas while also being the best prevention of relapse (Beck & Dozois, 2011). Despite CBT's goal of altering core beliefs and schemas, empirical evidence for this is lacking. In fact, the bulk of research supporting CBT's effectiveness for prevalent mental health issues mainly revolves around modifying negative automatic thoughts and occasionally dysfunctional intermediary assumptions rather than core beliefs (Westbrook, 2014). Dobson and Dobson (2017) propose that changes in negative core beliefs might occur gradually without direct modification, as clients continue to adopt new thoughts and behaviours over the long term or as they say "a chipping away".

Thus, despite having clear empirical evidence, when we look at how people improve, having a clear commitment to gradual and consistent progress is both practical and essential. That is, in CBT, "the way people get better is by making small changes in their thinking and behaviour every day" (Beck, 2021, p. 166). This is an important attitude for the client to accept and integrate into their lives. It is one of the many adaptive beliefs that may require exploration in therapy before treatment planning.

The Islāmically Modified Change Process

The Islāmic correlate to change processes can be the Hadīth narrated by Abu Huraira whereby the Messenger of Allāh, peace and blessings be upon him, said,

> Take up good deeds only as much as you are able, for the best deeds are those done regularly even if they are few.
>
> (Ibn Mājah (a))

Both Islāmic teaching and the CBT approach encourage individuals to avoid being overwhelmed by trying to achieve drastic changes all at once. Instead, they advocate for a step-by-step, consistent, and patient approach to positive transformation. Although this connection highlights how Islāmic principles can reinforce and complement psychological techniques, we can still go deeper.

The notion that persistent activity leads to change is pretty standard across therapies. The cliche practice makes perfect is not necessarily incorrect, except that "practice makes progress" is more accurate. This is relevant at the physical level (i.e. exercise), cognitive level (i.e. thought management), and at spiritual levels (i.e. prayer). The more one exercises, engages in metacognition, and prays, the higher the likelihood they are to be physically, psychologically, and spiritually healthy. However, if done without the knowledge of the structure of the body, exercising in a wrong way can lead to more harm than good, and being in a constant state of analysing one's thoughts can also be problematic. Finally, engaging in prayer as the Prophet (ﷺ) prayed is the best form of prayer and thus finding the right balance is key.

While the earlier Hadīth emphasises that small consistent deeds are preferred over inconsistent and large ones, it does not necessarily provide a direct mechanism for change. Thus the following Hadīth can be used to provide both a problem and change mechanisms model.

> Hudhaifa said: I heard the Messenger of Allāh (ﷺ) observing: Temptations will be presented to men's hearts as reed mat is woven stick by stick and any heart which is impregnated by them will have a black mark put into it, but any heart which rejects them will have a white mark put in it. The result is that there will become two types of hearts: one white like a white stone which will not be harmed by any turmoil or temptation, so long as the heavens and the earth endure; and the other black and dust-coloured like a vessel which is upset, not recognizing what is good or rejecting what is abominable, but being impregnated with passion.
>
> (Muslim (d))

This Hadīth is more comprehensive and provides both a pathological and change mechanisms model, with a focus on primary prevention of "shahawat" or temptations. If we conceptualised automatic thoughts as a type of cognitive temptation (or any other internal and unobservable process), it can be quite meaningful. For example, a thought record that includes these cognitive temptations can be used and even if shared with a non-Muslim therapist practising CBT can be worked on in therapy.

Furthermore, by providing a change mechanisms model, we can begin to synthesise other theories to assist in helping clients enhance their intrinsic motivation towards change. For example, the organismic integration theory (OIT), developed by Deci and Ryan (1985), explains how the internalisation process of extrinsically motivated behaviour changes from lower degrees of autonomy to higher ones to eventually become more of an internalised form of motivation. In OIT, external motivation is divided along a continuum of internalisation; simply put, from "mustivation to wantivation". This theory can provide the mechanisms required to shift a behaviour (e.g. prayer) from mustivation ("I have to pray") to wantivation ("I want to pray") through the facilitation of the three basic psychological needs. Perhaps, one of the reasons why a specific client may not feel fulfilled despite engaging in a highly religious activity is that they are operating against autonomy when they feel controlled by others. This can then be connected to the fundamental principle behind all actions from an Islāmic perspective – sincerity. Sincerity can be operationalised based on the following famous Hadīth, which is usually the first one mentioned in the primary compilations of Hadīth.

> Umar bin Al-Khattab (May Allāh be pleased with him), reported: The Messenger of Allāh (PBUH) said, "The deeds are considered by the intentions, and a person will get the reward according to their intention".
>
> (Bukhârî (d))

Islāmic Correlate to the Bio-Psycho-Social Model

Expanding the traditional bio-psycho-social model to also emphasise the spiritual and occupational domains provides a more comprehensive perspective on an individual's life. In Islām, the *maqasid* (objectives) of *Shar'iah* (Islāmic law) encompasses five main purposes: the preservation of religion, life, intellect, lineage, and property. These objectives can be conceptualised from an individual level of analysis, corresponding to the physical, psychological, social, occupational, and spiritual domains respectively (personal communication with Dr Jaser Auda, a scholar in Islāmic Maqasid). By integrating the Maqasid with the expanded domains of the bio-psycho-social model, a holistic framework emerges that recognises the interconnectedness of various aspects of an individual's life. This approach provides a comprehensive understanding of well-being and guides individuals to live balanced and fulfilling lives in accordance with their culture and religion.

However, one common critique of the bio-psycho-social model is which gets prioritised? From an Islāmic perspective, specific behaviours can be classified based on their degree of importance determined by whether the action is considered virtuous or sinful. This would be based on actions by omission or commission and thus functional or dysfunctional from a spiritual lens. That is, when deciding whether a certain action is acceptable or not according to Islāmic jurisprudence, there are five degrees of approval known as *ahkam*. The degrees are haram (forbidden resulting in sin by commission), *makrooh* (disliked – but no sin by commission but reward for omission), *mubah* (permissible – neither sinful nor rewarded), *mustahab* (encouraged – no sin for omission but reward for commission), and *wajib* (obligatory – reward for commission and sin for omission). Voluntary activities would fall under the *Mustahab* or encouraged category, but if the client believes it to be *wajib*, then they also accept that not doing it is a sin which in turn will have psychological implications. Thus, examining social roles and differentiating between what is considered obligatory and what is considered voluntary can be meaningful. Furthermore, specific religious activities that cause physical, psychological, social, or occupational harm could be examined with the client from a religious and spiritual lens rather than resorting to a value system outside of the client's worldview. This approach would be quite relevant when cultural practices disguised as religious require challenging.

Differentiating Culture and Religion

Culture and religion are intertwined aspects of an individual's identity, but it is essential to distinguish between them when considering mental health treatment. Culture encompasses a broader set of beliefs, values, norms, and practices shared by a specific group, whereas religion often refers to the spiritual beliefs and practices of an individual or community (Hodge, 2016). It is crucial to recognise that not all psychological experiences within a cultural or religious group can be attributed solely to either culture or religion, as they often interact and influence each other. Furthermore, which takes precedence if there is a conflict?

Walpole, McMillan, House, Cottrell, and Mir (2013) conducted a systematic review examining interventions for treating depression in Muslim patients. Their study analysed existing literature, focusing on qualitative and quantitative studies, as well as opinion pieces, and their review identified 25 studies that met the inclusion criteria. The findings revealed diverse beliefs about depression treatment among Muslims and highlighted contradictions in the advice given to address these beliefs. The review emphasised the need for high-quality research to improve understanding, modify therapies, and evaluate their effectiveness in treating depression in Muslim patients. They also provide several key recommendations based on their review that we will address throughout this book.

For example, they identified that distinctions between religious and cultural factors were often lacking, especially with respect to perceptions of the source and cure for depression. They clarify that interpreting depression as a "test" in Islāmic teachings might be beneficial and doesn't necessarily imply fatalism. However, the therapist needs to be attentive to when religious justifications are done in a fatalistic or dysfunctional fashion as opposed to a strong coping resource. Furthermore, they highlight that collaboration with religious experts within or outside mental health services is recommended, especially when supernatural explanations or misinterpretations of religious teachings contribute to depression. However, through IMCBT, one may be able to take an initial approach to addressing supernatural issues from both lenses using the same CBT techniques. These techniques are detailed in the next chapter with accompanying Islāmic correlates.

6 Islāmically Modified Cognitive Behavioural Therapy Techniques and Strategies

Techniques in psychotherapy can be broken down into specific and non-specific components (Amole, et al., 2017). Specific components are those that are theoretically grounded and often unique to a specific therapy. For example, in CBT, analysing the evidence for and against an automatic thought would be considered a specific component, whereas establishing a therapeutic alliance would be non-specific. The task force (Klepac et al., 2012) also identifies examples of evidence-based interventions that characterise behavioural and cognitive psychology rather than a definitive set of clinical skills. The following list includes all of these interventions, which have been ordered under the specific domain that they could fall under. Since interventions rarely focus on only one domain, this reordering is intended only for structure and not necessarily function and corresponds to the psychological. Furthermore, only the basic definitions of each are derived from the APA dictionary for your quick reference. They include the following.

Behavioural

Stimulus Control	A behavioural therapy technique that involves manipulating environmental cues to influence or change a specific behaviour.
Behavioural Activation	A therapeutic approach aimed at increasing engagement in positive and fulfilling activities to alleviate symptoms of depression or other mood disorders.
Extinction/Exposure Strategies	Methods used in behaviour therapy to reduce the frequency of unwanted behaviours by systematically removing or confronting the stimuli that trigger those behaviours.
Contingency Management	A behavioural therapy technique that reinforces desired behaviours through the use of rewards or consequences based on specific contingencies.
Shaping of Complex Chains of Behaviour	The process of gradually teaching and reinforcing a sequence of behaviours until a complex task or skill is achieved.

DOI: 10.4324/9781003364207-8

Cognitive

Defusion/Distancing	A component of acceptance and commitment therapy (ACT) that helps individuals detach from distressing thoughts and emotions, allowing them to respond more flexibly to life's challenges.
Modifying Cognitive Processes	Techniques like reappraisal, reframing, and restructuring used in CBT to change thought patterns and beliefs associated with emotional distress.
Modification of Core Cognitive Beliefs/ Tacit Knowledge Structures	A CBT strategy that involves challenging and altering deeply held beliefs and assumptions that contribute to psychological distress.
Enhancing Psychological Acceptance	A central concept in ACT that involves embracing difficult thoughts and emotions rather than struggling against them.

Affective, Physiological, Social, Occupational, and Pervasive Interventions

Emotion Regulation	The ability to recognise, understand, and manage one's own emotions effectively.
Distress Tolerance	The capacity to endure and cope with distressing emotions and situations without resorting to harmful or impulsive behaviours.
Arousal Reduction Strategies	Techniques such as relaxation training, biofeedback, hypnosis, and meditation used to reduce physiological and psychological arousal.
Interpersonal Skills Training	A form of therapy that focuses on improving communication and relationship-building skills, often used to address interpersonal problems.
Self-Management (Self-Monitoring/ Habit Reversal)	Strategies that empower individuals to take control of their behaviour by monitoring and changing habits or reactions.
Psychoeducation	Providing individuals with information and knowledge about mental health conditions, treatments, and coping strategies.
Homework	Assignments or tasks given to clients in therapy to practise and apply therapeutic techniques outside of sessions.

Stimulus Control: The Sleep 20 Intervention

In many of my sessions, when I explore sleep interventions for insomnia, one often used technique is what I call Sleep 20. That is, derived from CBT for insomnia, if the client has not fallen asleep within 20 minutes of lying in bed, they are to get out of bed, then come back when they are tired again. This technique prevents the problem from getting worse and is a type of stimulus control intervention. To facilitate this, I first ask if they listen to the Qur'ân before falling asleep. For those who do, I ask them to select a recitation that lasts about 20 minutes, and if it ends before sleeping, get up and leave the room. I would explain that this would be better than setting an alarm or constantly looking at the clock because if they did fall asleep and the alarm went off it would defeat the purpose. Furthermore, if they keep eyeing the clock, it'll likely cause more distress and keep them awake.

However, with one client in particular, when I asked her if she listens to the Qur'ân before falling asleep, she said "I don't think the Qur'ân should be used that way, it should be listened to and reflected upon". Thus, I did not continue with using the Qur'ân to facilitate the Sleep 20 intervention but simply explained the rationale behind the intervention. What this case brought to light for me is the importance of ensuring that any Islāmic intervention should be used in an appropriate Islāmic manner. The definition of appropriate may be subject to scholarly debate on any specific intervention, thus utilising the client's worldview and, by extension, what they deem appropriate is where we would derive our evidence.

Islāmically Modified Cognitive Techniques

Cognitive interventions are one of the key components of CBT. The objective of a cognitive intervention is reshaping thought patterns to promote positive emotions and behaviours. The task force outlines a set of cognitive-based techniques which include defusion/distancing, modifying cognitive processes, changing core cognitive beliefs, and enhancing psychological acceptance (Klepac et al., 2012). Defusion/distancing is a cognitive technique that involves creating distance or separation from distressing thoughts or emotions to reduce their impact and influence. Enhancing psychological acceptance are strategies aimed at increasing an individual's willingness to accept and embrace their thoughts, emotions, and experiences without judgement or attempts to control or avoid them, whereas cognitive modification strategies are intended to change or alter the pattern of thinking.

For example, modifying cognitive processes includes reappraisal, reframing, and restructuring. These cognitive techniques involve actively changing or altering how thoughts are perceived, interpreted, or processed to promote more adaptive and helpful thinking patterns. Modification of core cognitive beliefs/tacit knowledge structures is another cognitive intervention that targets and modifies deeply held core beliefs or underlying knowledge structures that may contribute to maladaptive thoughts, emotions, and behaviours. While each technique has its unique focus, they are interrelated within the context of CBT. Reappraisal often serves as a basic form of cognitive restructuring, as it encourages individuals to challenge and replace automatic negative thoughts with more rational ones. Reframing can encompass both reappraisal and restructuring techniques, as it involves shifting perspectives and altering emotional responses. Restructuring, on the other hand, delves deeper into identifying cognitive distortions and implementing systematic changes in thinking patterns. In essence, these techniques share the overarching goal of modifying cognitive processes to bring about changes in emotional responses and behaviours. While their specific applications may differ, the underlying principle remains consistent: altering cognitive patterns to foster positive change which makes them highly amenable to Islāmic modifications, and their biological correlates can be traced.

Biological Basis: Neuroplasticity and Emotion Regulation

Reappraisal's impact extends to the biological realm through its influence on neural pathways and emotion regulation. The process of reappraisal triggers neuroplasticity, a phenomenon where the brain's structure and function adapt in response to experiences (APA, n.d. (a)). As individuals consistently engage in reappraisal, neural connections associated with negative interpretations weaken while pathways linked to positive reappraisals strengthen. This neuroplastic change results in enhanced emotion regulation. Brain regions responsible for regulating emotions, such as the prefrontal cortex, become more adept at down regulating emotional responses to stressors, thus facilitating reduced anxiety, improved mood, and heightened emotional resilience.

The Islāmic Evidence

Despite the nature of the thought itself, viewing intrusive thoughts of any kind can be conceptualised as whispers from *shaytan* (devil). This is not to be confused with delusions or supernatural issues beyond the control of the client but rather, from an Islāmic perspective, is considered normal, and these whispers cannot be physically heard. The verse from the Qur'ân that identifies this is the following:

> *And if there comes to you from Satan an evil suggestion, then seek refuge in Allāh. Indeed, He is the Hearing, the Knowing.*
>
> (Ya-Sin 36:41)

Furthermore, this Hadīth and the associated verse can be used to provide the rationale for focusing on the nature of the thoughts while also encouraging metacognition or thinking about thinking.

> Abdullah ibn Mas'ud reported: The Messenger of Allāh, peace and blessings be upon him, said, "Verily, Satan has influence with the son of Adam and the angel has influence. As for the influence of Satan, he promises evil and denies the truth. As for the influence of the angel, he promises goodness and affirms the truth. Whoever finds this goodness, let him know that

> it is from Allāh and let him praise Allāh. Whoever finds something else, let him seek refuge in Allāh from the accursed Satan". Then, the Prophet ﷺ recited the verse, "Satan threatens you with poverty and commands evil, but Allāh promises you forgiveness and favor from him".
>
> (al-Tirmidhī(a))

Another Hadīth that can be used in conjunction with cognitive interventions is the following:

> Al-Hasan ibn Ali reported: The Messenger of Allāh (ﷺ), said: Leave what makes you doubt for what does not make you doubt. Verily, truth brings peace of mind and falsehood sows doubt.
>
> (al-Tirmidhī(b))

This can be used to explain to Muslim clients the connection between uncertainty and anxiety by exploring the concept of doubt. Furthermore, it can provide the client with the mechanisms for "peace of mind" as being connected to thinking based on evidence rather than just a broad category of mental health.

With respect to reframing, the following Hadīth can be quite effective.

> Aisha reported: The Messenger of Allāh (ﷺ) said to me one day, "O Aisha, do you have anything to eat?" She said, "O Messenger of Allāh, I have nothing". The Prophet said, "Then I am fasting".
>
> (Muslim (e))

Although this Hadīth is often used to provide evidence on the jurisprudence of voluntary fasting (i.e. related to intentions), it can also be used to further enhance the positive view of reframing an event that can be perceived as negative into a more positive outcome, especially to prevent social conflict. This Hadīth can be used with a client to open the door to discussing the rationale behind both reframing and reappraisal. Furthermore, it can also allow for a deeper discussion around the Prophet Muhammad's (ﷺ) noble characteristics of patience facilitated by his profound cognitive flexibility.

Rumination: Problem-Solving the Past and Coping With the Future

Problem-solving the past and coping with the future is a cognitive conceptualisation of a pathological and change mechanisms model I developed. The following provides an example of what a cognitive conceptualisation write-up might look like.

After conducting the functional analysis for the client's depressive symptoms, it is apparent that rumination serves as an important factor in increasing feelings of both hopelessness and helplessness and often resulting in reduced activities. When the rumination occurs prior to falling asleep, it can also be implicated in the client's sleep disturbances. The interaction between the client's rumination and their depressed mood appear to be exacerbating both. That is, while the client is in a depressed mood, they are more vulnerable to rumination. In turn, this rumination tends to further exacerbate the negative emotions and thoughts contributing to the depressed mood. The impact of the client's rumination is also likely contributing to feelings of helplessness. That is, this style of thinking is often associated with a temporary paralysis in critical thinking and problem-solving skills. As the client becomes so preoccupied with the problem, they struggle to move past this cycle of negative thoughts. As a result, they are likely to believe that they are powerless.

I explained to the client that what he is experiencing is what I call the "Problem solving the past-Coping with the Future" and that the goal is to reverse this as problem-solving which can possibly influence (the future) and coping with what he cannot (the past). Focusing on shifting the client's negative self-talk from counterproductive (e.g. rumination) to productive (adaptive self-reflection) was established as one major objective. Thus, an associated goal in the CBT intervention for depression was to reduce the frequency, intensity, and duration of the client's rumination and ultimately aiming to replace rumination altogether with adaptive self-reflection. Given the client's deep commitment to Islām, it was necessary and advantageous to integrate Islāmic principles and practices into the conceptualisation of his problem.

Adaptive Self-Reflection and Interrogatives

Adaptive self-reflection can be conceptualised as the opposite of rumination. Instead of focusing on abstract and generalised aspects of the problem they cannot change, in adaptive self-reflection, focus is placed on concrete parts of a challenge along with progress they can make. Achieving this goal can also be supplemented with problem-solving therapy strategies to maximise outcomes. We discussed this cycle from a CBT perspective and how thoughts influence emotions and behaviours. As the client recalls negative experiences, how they interpret what happened to them in the past, they are more likely to interpret current situations more negatively contributing to less hopefulness in the future.

In order to help the client overcome the "problem solving the past and coping with the future" problem, identifying the abstract questions that are involved in the client's negative self-talk was important. These questions are often in the form of "why me" or "why can't I get better" and are common in keeping the client in the rumination cycle. Rather, the basic intervention was to practise with the client in shifting the "interrogatives" from "why" to any of the other possibilities; for example, "when" will I get better or "what" do I need to do to get better. Furthermore, the difference between a problem-centred style of thinking and a solution-focused mindset was linked to this type of shift in thinking. Although the problem-centred mindset may be useful at times when the client is seeking insight into a problem, it is not always amenable to problem-solving (hence, why problem-solving in the past is beyond their control).

The client will work towards trying to catch themselves when they fall into the "why" trap and shift to any other interrogative. With respect to problems in the past that the client tends to ruminate on, it is hoped that the "problem solving the past" concept will serve to remind them to engage in solution-focused strategies. When attempting to begin problem-solving, they tend to quickly regress to feeling that they cannot do it. Thus, committing to one specific activity can be the first step in a series of steps towards overcoming rumination.

Islāmic Foundation for Rumination

Distraction is often an effective intervention for rumination (Winch, 2013). In addition, one can employ Islāmic principles to help support the client to strengthen their ability to prevent dysfunctional thoughts such as "if only I did something else, the outcome would be different". In one session, I requested from a highly religious and practising client to not make supplications or *dua*. On the face of the record, this can be construed as being quite insensitive. But in this case, the act of *dua* served as a constant reminder and part of her rumination on the past; thus, it was not only aggravating her problem but was also not being done in the proper manner.

Abu Huraira reported: The Messenger of Allāh (ﷺ) said, "Call upon Allāh with certainty that He will answer you. Know that Allāh will not answer the supplication of a heart that is unmindful and distracted" (al-Tirmidhī (c)).

When she was convinced that she was not making *dua* in the proper way, I provided Islāmic evidence on a better alternative, which in this case, was *thikr* or the remembrance of Allāh citing the following Hadīth Qudsi.

> Whoever is distracted by remembrance of Me from asking of Me, I shall give him the best of that which I give to those who ask.
>
> (al-Tirmidhī (d))

There is a comprehensive Hadīth that can have a great deal of transformative benefits beyond simple distraction. It reads:

> The stronger believer is better and more beloved to Allāh than the weak believer, although both are good. Strive to seek that which will benefit you and do not feel helpless. If something overwhelms you, then say:

QaddarAllāh, wa ma sha'a fa'al (It is the decree of Allāh and what He wills He does). And beware of (saying) "If only", for "If only" opens the door to Satan.

(Ibn Mājah (b))

This Hadīth not only normalises being weak and acknowledges how helpless people can become but also encourages functional behaviour (strive to seek that which will benefit you). Additionally, to invoke the self-statement that "It is the decree of Allāh and what He wills He does" can be adaptive. Furthermore, the caution not to say "if only" is where the problem-solving of the past problem finds its Islāmic roots.

Islāmic Foundation: "Why" to "When"

Shifting from "why" to "when" questions can facilitate hope and change, even in the darkest of circumstances, by redirecting focus towards actionable steps and future possibilities. When someone is in a very dark place, the constant rumination on "why" can intensify feelings of despair and hopelessness. However, introducing "when" questions can provide a sense of direction, purpose, and potential for improvement.

The most notable example of this in the holy Qur'ân is found in the following verse:

- *Or think you that you will enter Paradise without such (trials) as came to those who passed away before you? They were afflicted with severe poverty and ailments and were so shaken that even the Messenger and those who believed along with him said, "When (will come) the Help of Allāh? Yes! Certainly, the Help of Allāh is near!"*

(Al-Baqarah 2: 124)

The scholarly interpretation of this verse can be used in multiple ways to provide interventions that facilitate hope by shifting our thinking away from a sense of hopelessness and facilitating meaningful, consistent action. For example, trust in Allāh emphasises the importance of sincere faith, righteous actions, and seeking Allāh's help while also encouraging believers to fulfil their obligations, follow the Prophet's (ﷺ) example, and engage in acts of worship (positive actions).

The interpretation of the verse also highlights the rewards of patience and steadfastness in difficult times while also encouraging the importance of preparation and planning (coping and problem-solving), reminding individuals of the power of supplication and constant remembrance of Allāh and stressing the importance of combining trust in Allāh with practical efforts (reliance and action).

Thus, the integration of psychological theories and interventions with Islāmic correlates showcases the potential for cross-disciplinary collaboration and adaptation to cultural and religious contexts. This approach not only enhances the credibility of psychological practices but also promotes a more inclusive and effective approach to mental health and well-being. Thus, it is not sufficient to only learn the theories and evidence to support CBT, rather it is essential to critically appraise the evidence and examine the underlying mechanisms and processes. When this can be linked back to the biological and neurological correlates, it provides a heightened degree of credibility. Furthermore, by deconstructing empirically supported interventions into their specific components, it becomes possible to gain a deeper understanding of why and how these therapies are effective for specific clients in specific contexts, highlighting the role of biological, cognitive, and affective factors (Hoffmann & Hayes, 2019) and thus facilitate the process of being able to make modifications with fidelity and flexibility.

Islāmically Modified Interpersonal Skills Training

In the following case, the client and her mother were attending therapy due to serious communication problems that can be summarised as intergenerational divide issues. After an in-depth assessment, it was agreed that the mother was concerned about her daughter's current infatuation with certain topics that she felt contradict Islām, whereas the daughter, who is a devout Muslim, explains that she brings these controversial issues up to her mom because she has no one else to speak to. Although the mother exhibited generalised anxiety disorder symptoms, the daughter was diagnosed with major depressive disorder. Since they came together, I shifted from individual treatment to a couples approach with a focus on communication.

Using humour, as will be explained, can be quite meaningful. However, in this case, it was not the humour that facilitated progress, rather the therapeutic alliance that I had with both the mother and the daughter allowed me to challenge both of their dysfunctional thinking without either feeling that they were being attacked. Furthermore, the mother would speak in Arabic and the daughter would speak in English (despite understanding Arabic very well).

Mahdi: Do you believe in aliens?

Daughter: Hahaha, you know, I was saying that to my mom and she got upset.

Mom: I didn't get upset, I was telling you . . .

Mahdi: Let me stop you for a second. What is the Islāmic opinion on believing in aliens?

Mom: Uhhh, I don't know.

Mahdi: Isn't Adam from Jannah and we are from Adam? Doesn't that make us aliens?

Both the mother and the daughter burst into laughter which allowed me to continue to work on aligning their frame of reference when communicating while indirectly addressing the mother's anxiety around her daughter and the daughter's sense of loneliness. In a follow-up session, I utilised one Hadīth that framed the entire intervention.

Mahdi: I noticed a pattern when you speak to her. You know, you say a great thing about her, but then you add "but". You have to watch your "buts" [I take a quick glance at the daughter who I can tell found it humorous].
Mother: Yeah you're right I do that. But MashAllāh, she has so many good . . .
Mahdi: Ha, there it goes again, you just said it.
Mother: (laughs)
Mahdi: Think about it this way, what did the *Mushrikeen* (pagan worshippers) at the time of Muhammad PBUH used to say in their *talbiyah* (chanting when orbiting around the Kaabah). The same thing we say today, BUT they would add the Shirk (partnership with Allāh) by adding that one word – "except".
Mother: SubhanAllāh, you're right.

I was still not convinced that this was sufficient as it would only serve to stop her from saying. Rather, I wanted her to analyse her thoughts before speaking, and thus I introduced a model for her to follow referencing the Hadīth "whoever believes in Allāh and the last day, let them speak good or stay silent" (Bukhârî (e)).

Mahdi: Speak good or stay silent – say it, [the good thing] then in a different communication all together say the criticism. But if you want to criticise, you are her mother, you can, but you can't use the compliment sandwich here – you know like
"I like that you read, though I do have concerns about the content. Nonetheless, I'm pleased with your critical thinking skills." You are a good thinker.

We then identified one topic they recently discussed to use as a case example to practise the new skills.

Daughter: Darwinism
Mother: (noticeably distraught)
Mahdi: You know it doesn't have a purpose right?
Daughter: Huh?
Mahdi: Yeah, no, purpose. According to Darwinism, we live, we eat, we reproduce, we die. That's it. It's not supposed to have a purpose; just an explanation.

Daughter: Yeah, I don't really believe it anyway.
Mahdi: I mean some of the points can be very useful, but how do you think they [Darwinian] would view racism? Survival of the fittest?

I then explained a point that I felt perhaps provided a little more empathy for her mother while also maintaining respect for the client's experiences with oppression. This was a result of the daughter bringing up social justice and the eugenics movement, which is perhaps one of the most heinous issues that the field of psychology has endorsed (see APA, 2021 apology for details). After following up with the mother, she explained that she really wanted that type of guidance for her daughter, but I reminded her that therapy is not advice and that we should begin to look for a mentor for her to be able to share her ideas and thoughts without feeling like she is going to get in trouble.

7 What Does Not Work in Therapy

Learning From Naimah's Journey

Whereas ample evidence points to the essential practice of adapting to the client's preferences, culture, and religion, there are still those who are either unwilling or unable to do so. Based on the review by Norcross and Karpiak (2023), therapists should emphasise the importance of avoiding rigid adherence to treatment manuals. Therapists should be open to professional self-doubt, align their approach with client needs, and maintain humility. These stances allow for better empathy from therapists and prevent patients from feeling unheard, unappreciated, or disengaged from therapy. In the following case, the client was distraught after feeling offended by her occupational therapist for saying, "can't you just put your religion aside for once". This case demonstrates an example of perhaps the antithesis of evidence-based practice.

The Case of Naimah

Mrs Naimah is a highly educated 40-year-old mother who has been very resilient her whole life and currently struggling after a motor vehicle accident. Severe pain has left her with a medical leave of absence from work and embroiled in a challenging case as she is suing the other party and has been feeling her insurance is not on her side. She was referred to a clinic to see a physiotherapist, occupational therapist, and chiropractor by the insurance company. Despite her often aggressive appearance, she is quite passive when it comes to dealing with authority, especially those of the dominant society.

Furthermore, she is married to a convert to Islām who is Caucasian. She often has him speak to them to make sure her point is understood as she assumes their behaviour is based on a negative bias of her culture, despite her speaking fluent English and has lived in Canada most of her life. She doesn't feel they take her seriously, and she explained that she is just waiting for the original physiotherapist to return so she can continue with them (they had gone on maternity leave, and the clinic that is part of the same umbrella organisation that was closer to her house no longer had enough staff so she was transferred across town). The last straw that broke the proverbial camel's

DOI: 10.4324/9781003364207-9

back was the inspiration for this chapter, namely the statement "can't you just put your religion aside for once". During one of our sessions, she mentioned that the clinic where she undergoes physiotherapy and occupational therapy suggested she consult their psychologist. She explained to them that she is already seeing one. She explained that they repeatedly asked on multiple occasions to switch therapists, and each time she would get frustrated and explain why she does not want to. In one instance, she explained to me that she listed the following six points.

1 I have been treating him since the beginning and I am happy there.
2 I am benefitting.
3 He understands my culture.
4 He speaks my language.
5 He is available for me anytime I need him.
6 My physician specifically recommended him.

When I asked her why she stayed if she was not happy there, she explained that she felt she had no choice. If she changes it would jeopardise her treatment and likely cause a major challenge with the insurance. Despite my attempts to have her examine the evidence for her assumptions, each suggestion I would make was quickly challenged with reasonable justification leading me to conclude that even by attempting to have her look at alternative explanations, I was likely invalidating her terrible experience. I offered to contact the occupational therapist to discuss the matter, but the client declined and said, "I am just waiting for the old physiotherapist to return and then I'm leaving them altogether."

Therapeutic Alliance: Bonds, Consensus, Empathy, and Positive Regard

What works in therapy is based on extensive research which is summarised in Norcross and Karpiak (2023). Chief amongst the list is the therapeutic alliance. The therapeutic relationship between a therapist and a client is a crucial factor in predicting patient outcomes in therapy. The therapeutic alliance, which encompasses the emotional bond between patient and therapist and their collaborative agreement on therapy goals and methods, is another critical factor. Extensive research, summarised in Norcross and Karpiak (2023), highlights the significance of the therapeutic alliance in therapy, emphasising the vital role of the emotional bond and collaborative agreement between therapist and client, with therapist attitudes and behaviours, including empathy and positive regard, being crucial factors predicting positive patient outcomes. Many of these factors are likely the reasons for why she made the testimony about me.

Furthermore, when alliance ruptures occur, characterised by periods of poor relatedness, therapists' efforts to repair these ruptures are moderately associated with positive client outcomes. Thus, by recognising that my attempt at providing the occupational therapist with the benefit of the doubt was likely to offend the client, I immediately retracted and explained that I agreed the behaviour was quite unprofessional and demonstrated empathy rather than continuing to challenge her views.

What Does Not Work?

This case study exposes extreme ethical violations and raises concerns about the effectiveness of the client's treatment with the occupational therapist based on meta-analytic data. Although ruptures are often due to unintentional acts, there is a range of behaviours that simply do not work and can even be harmful to clients. Norcross and Karpiak (2023) provide a summary of the research uncovering these factors. These include low therapist empathy, poor therapeutic alliances, incongruence between a therapist's words and actions, and disregarding alliance ruptures. All of these factors are likely present in the case.

The findings from research also identify harmful therapist behaviours, such as rigidly adhering to treatment manuals, overconfidence, hostility, confrontational styles, and cultural arrogance. Furthermore, mandating the use of specific treatment protocols and prioritising manualised treatments over relationship factors can also be detrimental to client outcomes. The main issue was that the interventions used by the occupational therapist with respect to sleep focused on clearing her mind before sleeping and not thinking about anything. The client responded, "but I have to do my prayers before I sleep", to which the therapist responded, "can't you put your religion aside for once". Had this been the first session with her, it could have been a simple misunderstanding of the importance that the client places on her faith. But this was not the first session. The client explained to me that during the first session with her, she was asked about coping strategies with pain and sleep, and the client clearly stated how she draws on her faith. She explained that she engages in a regular religious routine before sleeping and recites Qur'ân and thikr until she falls asleep. The occupational therapist praised her for this and was excited to know she had strong coping resources.

Thus, my analysis of this case is that given the lack of progress she was making, the therapist was likely trying to rigidly apply her approach to sleep interventions and failed to recognise the importance of the client's religious rituals. It was quite odd to me as the Federation of Occupational Therapists appear to place much more emphasis on spirituality than the field of psychology. That is, they clearly identify spirituality not only in their code of ethics but also in their practice standards. Norcross and Karpiak (2023) provide irrefutable evidence to assert that therapist behaviours that blame, criticise, or show hostility towards patients can lead to worse outcomes. When the therapist's assumptions about clients do not align with their experiences, it hinders the collaborative nature of therapy. The client felt they were blaming her for not progressing and despite regressing, rather than reaching out to cultural brokers or trying to identify how to incorporate the client's faith in her treatment, she instead showed hostility.

Part III

Practice

8 The First Session

Welcoming With Peace and Hospitality

Seeing a psychologist for the first time can be anxiety provoking due to the sheer uncertainty of what to expect or many other uncontrollable factors the guest may have experienced. In the realm of relationships, the concept of hospitality takes centre stage as an invaluable tool for fostering respect and building connections with people. Imagine entering a space where you're instantly greeted with warmth and genuine kindness. This experience is what we aim to create in therapy, a safe space where clients feel acknowledged, valued, and deeply respected from the very moment they step in. Starting from a common phrase and value amongst Muslims, *salamu alaykum* or peace be upon you. Beyond the words, it is the spirit of peace that is a hallmark of this principle and hospitality. However, imagine walking into a place for the first time, and you are greeted with a request to sign a waiver form, you know, "in case something goes wrong". Even if they try to convince you that it is just standard practice, whether one adopts a collectivist or individualistic approach, it would still not feel hospitable. Although this is common in the practice of psychotherapy, it may send the wrong message. In this chapter, I argue that the informed consent process is a golden opportunity to better understand the client, establish bonds of trust and respect, and challenge any negative pre-existing notions of therapy.

With Muslim clients, you can align your practice with the teachings of Islām that emphasise the significance of hospitality, symbolising a profound commitment to treating guests with utmost care and consideration. Even if Muslims are not familiar with the scripture, they are often familiar with the general principle of hospitality. The Prophet Muhammad (ﷺ) once said, "Whoever believes in Allāh and the Last Day should serve his guest generously" (Bukhârî (e)). This principle resonates deeply with the approach taken in my practice and has demonstrated multiple benefits.

First, it can be looked at as the core of respecting the dignity of peoples, a fundamental ethical principle in psychology. Second, it can greatly contribute to establishing a strong therapeutic alliance while reducing anxiety around the process. By explaining to Muslim clients that they are guests and we are their hosts, it can activate a sense of familiarity and alleviate

DOI: 10.4324/9781003364207-11

any feelings of being a stranger. This chapter also addresses common challenges in the initial phase of counselling, including stigma and building rapport over the phone. During the COVID-19 pandemic, most sessions were conducted over the phone. This posed multiple challenges to demonstrating hospitality, and thus different strategies needed to be employed. I will demonstrate how I use culturally responsive humour in a structured way to not only establish rapport quickly but also assess the degree of Islāmic knowledge and commitment of the client. The case examples used in this chapter are with Arab-only speaking clients who have never seen a psychologist, and it was unclear what their preference or level of religiosity was. The chapter introduces an Islāmic intervention that can be used in the first 30 seconds with the client in person or over the phone with promising outcomes.

Informed Consent Process

Based on the principles of anxiety and uncertainty management theory (Gudykunst, 2005), the absence of such knowledge can lead to higher levels of uncertainty. Uncertainty is directly and positively related to anxiety, thus as uncertainty levels are higher so are anxiety levels. A high degree of uncertainty leads to fear, which could lead to maladaptive behaviours such as escape or avoidance. At the biological level, this includes the activation of the fight/flight response, and thus anxiety management not only includes relaxation to reduce the physiological arousal, but there needs to also be cognitive strategies to reduce uncertainty.

One way of providing the rational to the client could be:

Mahdi: The Prophet (ﷺ) said the cure for ignorance is enquiry. It seems that because this is new to you, there is a lot of uncertainty or things you do not know. When this happens, we tend to make assumptions without any evidence. So why don't we identify all the questions you may have and get them answered one by one. Does that sound like something you would like to do?

This often leads to further understanding of the client's worldview based on the questions they pose in the moment and about the moment. Furthermore, confidentiality questions may come up directly or indirectly. For example, in one case, the client seemed quite apprehensive about sharing any information regarding her problem as she had recently gotten into a divorce and was under the false impression that by feeling depressed it may somehow indicate she is an unfit mother. Although this may not be accurate, it is nonetheless her perspective and required careful attention. Thus, in this case (and many other ones), I quickly shift into discussing the informed consent process beginning with confidentiality.

Informed consent, confidentiality, and anonymity are of paramount importance in respecting the dignity of clients. The informed consent process does not end with a signature on a piece of paper (although that may be part of it); rather it is an ongoing process. Although the signature implies a contractual agreement, it is in no way a substitute for the essential process of ensuring that the guest is clear on what they are consenting to. Thus, despite signing the document, it is still very important to use this as an opportunity to strengthen the relationship and establish bonds of trust and respect.

When discussing issues of confidentiality and anonymity, I find it important to go beyond professional ethical standards and incorporate evidence from Islāmic sources to bolster Muslim clients' confidence that what is said in the room, stays in the room. With many clients, especially ones that are quite reluctant to discuss their presenting concern, I add that breaking confidentiality would not only be a professional catastrophe, but from an Islāmic perspective, it would land the therapist under the category of "having three signs of a hypocrite". This was explained from one Prophetic saying in which Muhammad (ﷺ) said:

> The signs of a hypocrite are three, even if they fast and pray and claim to be a Muslim. When they speak they lie, when they give a promise they break it, and when they are trusted they are treacherous.
>
> (Bukhârî (f))

I have found this additional information to be quite effective in helping the client to feel a sense of peace and safety – fundamental features of the principle of *sallam*. One running theme throughout this book is that establishing the relationship is essential as a first step; thus, jumping too quickly into interventions or assessment can rupture the relationship. For example, imagine, instead of reassuring the client that everything remains confidential, I had challenged her catastrophising and tried to logically challenge her misinformation. I have heard from clients before that they decided to terminate during the informed consent process (psychologically, as they remained for the rest of the session and never returned) simply because the therapist (who was also a Muslim) spent too much time speaking about limits of confidentiality around apprehending children if they are in danger, despite the presenting concern having no indication of abuse or relationship issues with children.

This brings up a point on judgement with respect to informed consent and the limits to confidentiality. Also, how to do them without losing sight of the most important person to consider in all matters of ethical dilemmas, the client always comes first. Although legal issues may trump ethical ones at times in our profession, it is important to know these policies and laws of your regulatory body and state/province. To reiterate, start with the principle of *sallam*, aiming to have the client feel like they are in a safe haven when they are with you. Evidence clearly suggests that religiously adapted interventions not only provide better therapeutic outcomes but also tend to enhance the therapeutic alliance early on more than the standard application in trials using CBT (Koenig et al., 2016). However, the differential effects seem to disappear over time, providing further justification for developing a model of adaptation with an emphasis on building and maintaining the therapeutic alliance during the initial moments of meeting the client.

9 Structuring the Session and the Islāmically Modified Mood Check

Utilising appropriate culturally responsive humour has been effective in enhancing the therapeutic alliance and outcomes (Sarink & García-Montes, 2023). Sarink and García-Montes conducted a systematic review to examine the impact of humour interventions in psychotherapy on depression and anxiety levels in adult clients. The review provides valuable insights into the potential benefits of humour-based interventions in addressing depression and anxiety within psychotherapy. Despite the need for further research, they identified that different research proposed varied perspectives on how humour can be utilised in therapy to challenge distorted thinking, enhance therapeutic relationships, or improve well-being.

Humour has the potential to create a positive and comfortable atmosphere in therapy, reducing tension and anxiety that clients may feel during sessions. When used appropriately, humour can break down barriers, build rapport between the therapist and client, and establish a sense of trust. This sets the stage for more open communication and a stronger therapeutic alliance. Appropriate humour should validate the client, be grounded in their worldview, and move the dialogue forward, whereas inappropriate humour can be disrespectful to the dignity of the client, severely rupture the therapeutic relationship, and kill the conversation. The purpose of these highly nuanced exchanges resulting in hearty chuckles are not to entertain the client for therapeutic purposes but rather to purposefully enter the therapeutic terrain with them. The dangers of common Islāmic concepts being unintentionally used as invalidating conversation killers are heightened when humour is applied. Thus, the difference between appropriate and inappropriate humour is crucial.

Using the client's frame of reference is key to the use of humour, which, if done correctly, can contribute to the therapeutic relationship by creating a sense of connection, empathy, and mutual understanding that allows the client to feel safe, heard, and valued. Furthermore, humour may be able to provide a new perspective on issues, helping clients reframe their thoughts and gain insights. It encourages cognitive flexibility and promotes the ability to see situations from different angles. This can lead to "Ah-Ha" moments of clarity, where clients gain deeper self-awareness and understanding.

DOI: 10.4324/9781003364207-12

Language Matching

Language is intimately connected to culture. It is an important way in which cultural meanings are shared, and it can be difficult to communicate certain meanings without the original words or phrases in which they emerged. Certain concepts germane to the lived reality of a Muslim client may not be easily expressed if they are not in the same language in which they emerged. Given the direct connection between language and culture, language matching or integrating language and culture into counselling is one practice that can enhance deeper understanding and validation for a client (Seto & Forth, 2020). A simple welcoming of the client to choose the language they want to use and at any time they choose to use it during therapy facilitates the counselling process and enhances the client's sense of peace and comfort. This includes embracing language switching when clients feel more comfortable using their first language for self-expression.

What I also find meaningful is to use their own language (Urdu, Somali, and others) or dialect in Arabic to represent the irrational concept of "crazy". However, language matching extends far beyond just humour and is often one of the main reasons I receive most of the Arab-speaking referrals. Here, dynamic bilingualism as a theme extends beyond just the language but also into the worldview of the client.

Humour and Alleviating Stigma

It's quite usual for Muslim guests (and various other cultural groups I work with) to carry the perception that seeking help from a psychologist implies being "crazy". After asking the client what language they would prefer we speak in, in many cases, I still notice a reluctance to open up or observe their non-verbal behaviours as an indication that they are not comfortable.

Mahdi: Is this the first time you see a psychologist?
Guest: Yes!
Mahdi: I'm curious, what did you think when they referred you to me?
Guest: . . . ahhh
Mahdi: Let me guess, you probably said to yourself, "*Shoo, ana mish majnoonah* (what, I am not crazy)"
Guest: (Bursts out in laughter as the Ha-Ha enables the Ah-Ha) Yah, Yah!

From here, there are usually multiple pathways. For example, in some instances, I may explain what they can expect in therapy in a manner that makes the therapeutic process seem as though it is something already inherent in their worldview. Or, I can normalise the emotions they are feeling by first asking them to share more about how they are currently feeling and what they view as the reason for the referral. The significance of using humour varies depending on the context, but overall, it holds value. In other cases, clients have said "no, I didn't think that at all, I was actually looking forward to coming". At this point, there is no need to continue with any humour as it would indicate that the client is not high in reactance or reluctance.

How the Client Sees the World

When applied to non-native English speakers, technical jargon can lead to periods of poor relatedness despite the client's level of intelligence. Thus, language matching is an important skill to develop which can be enhanced by being able to communicate the rationale behind interventions and change mechanisms in different ways that reflect the client's preferences, culture, and/or religion. However, what I have found quite meaningful is, when possible, to utilise technical language that the client is quite familiar with rather than just keeping the language too basic.

For example, one of my clients was a data scientist and quite familiar with computer hardware. Thus, explaining the information processing model behind CBT was not only seamless in the initial sessions but also utilised within the case conceptualisation for the client to be able to see the connection of his thoughts with other phenomena. Furthermore, it helped to alleviate some apprehension about taking medication which was not due to any side-effects or stigma but rather was quite foreign to him. In one session, the client had been referred to a psychiatrist to modify his medication. He had comorbid chronic pain, anxiety, and depression. When he was told about one medication that can address all three (Cymbalta), he thought it was too good to be true and dismissed it altogether. He was on the fence about it, and as we discussed it further, he arrived at the conclusion that it was "like a two-processor computer; one to manage one set of processes and the other to manage the others". Furthermore, I added that we tend to only get our computers diagnosed and serviced when they no longer function efficiently. This allowed for a wealth of opportunities to discuss his challenges at a deeper level. This was also then connected to the impairment in social and occupational domains and led us into the Islāmic spiritual domain by asking him, "I wonder if we can look at the spiritual side of things from the same dual processing computer lens".

Creative Strategies Using Humour to Reframe and Open Dialogue

Telepsychology involves providing psychological services using various telecommunication technologies (APA, 2013). One main issue that requires careful consideration is whether or not establishing a strong therapeutic alliance is possible over the phone. Without the many in-person strategies associated with demonstrating hospitality to the client/guest, trying out different approaches for alliance-building using telepsychology is necessary. In the next section, I will present the "Haha to Aywaa" intervention as one that has demonstrated ongoing promise across a range of diverse Muslim clients.

From Haha to Aywaa (Ah-Ha)

Aywa, means yes in some Arabic dialects. But when the last letter is elongated, it is colloquially akin to an "AH-HA" or "that's right" moment. This temporary mental shift has clinical utility, especially in moving the therapeutic dialogue forward.

Mahdi: *Sallamu Alaykum, Alhamdulillah ala Al Salamah* (A colloquial phrase literally translated as Thank God for your safety but means a lot more).
Client: *Wa alaykum al Sallam, Alhamdulillah.*
Mahdi: *Alhamdulillah Ala al Khayr wal Shar* (This is a statement that reflects the fundamental belief of Muslims related to fate and destiny and is translated as Thank God for the Good and the Bad).

At this point, their response indicates to me what level of knowledge they have but not their degree of religiosity as most Arabs will acquiesce, and their response could be cultural. However, when they add certain other terms, it provides further information on their level of knowledge. Furthermore, it is also important to note how this can lead to a type of conversation killer of shaming the client for complaining. Thus, the phrase I follow up with which has reached the level of being an effective strategy for hundreds of clients is:

Mahdi: *Hatti al shar* (Give me the bad).

I find this technique to be quite effective with most clients and serves to enhance the therapeutic relationship, and provides the client with validation, and for those who may feel that speaking about their problems is a type of sin or violation of the concept of fate and decree.

Islāmically Modified Mood Check

This can also be carried throughout therapy as an initial structure for the beginning of the session. For example, often in CBT, the sessions are structured beginning with a mood check (Beck, 2021). An Islāmically modified mood check could be to first ask them how they are doing, to which they will most likely respond with *Alhamdulillah (*praise be to Allāh).

Mahdi: How are you feeling today?
Client: (long sigh followed by) *Alhamdulillah*
Mahdi: Sounds like it's an *Alhamdulillah Ala Al Shar* (for the bad) type of day.
Client: Hahah, yeah it is, how did you know?
Mahdi: You know that deep sigh you made, it is your body forcing you to take a deep breath. I'd like to discuss deep breathing with you if you don't mind.

This type of mood check is especially useful when conducting telepsychology where not being able to see the client means we must pay extra careful attention to specific utterances and often find it difficult to catch non-verbal cues. Furthermore, silence in order to allow the client to process and reflect can also be challenging. For example, if the silence is too long, the client may ask, "are you still there" which could be an indication that the client does not feel you are present. Another use of this approach is to use it to allow the client to decide which direction they want to take the session in. But caution needs to be taken as the likelihood that they still retain feelings that they should not speak about bad things may still be lingering.

Mahdi: Which do you want to focus on, *khayr* (good) or *shar* (bad)?
Client: Let's focus on the *khayr*, always.
Mahdi: You know, sometimes it's important to also address the *shar* (bad). Do you ever get irritated when you talk about a problem and they tend to try to get you to "look on the bright-side"?
Client: Hahah, yeah all the time.
Mahdi: It's called toxic positivity, and I want to make sure we don't do that here.

The purpose of these highly nuanced exchanges resulting in hearty chuckles was not to entertain the client for therapeutic purposes but rather to purposefully enter the therapeutic terrain with them and can thus be highly effective if used properly while also being meaningful in structuring the session.

10 Islāmically Modified Case Conceptualisation

It is quite common for me to hear Muslim clients refer to their faith as their coping strategy in a variety of diverse ways.

Mahdi: What have you been doing to cope with this?
Client: I have been turning to my *deen* (faith).
Mahdi: What does that mean to you?
Client: I have been reading the Qur'ân and listening to Islāmic lectures.

How to integrate this into their treatment requires a strong case conceptualisation that integrates faith into a deeper understanding of the problems and matched solutions. Easden & Kazantzis (2018) conducted a systematic review of the use of case conceptualisation in CBT. They found that despite the paramount importance of this practice in matching interventions with the client's needs, there still remains a major gap in how it is done and its implications on therapeutic outcomes. One of the reasons this challenge may remain is that the uniqueness of each case conceptualisation may resemble the uniqueness of the client. That is, when adapting the therapeutic approach to the client's religion or spirituality, these adaptations of psychotherapy can be "as unique as each patient who walks through the door" (Captari et al., 2018, p. 1940). Thus, beginner therapists should not fret if they find that they have yet to master a deep level of case conceptualisation in general, particularly when adapting to the client's preferences, culture, and religion.

Case conceptualisation skills facilitate the synthesis of multiple forms of clinical data, differential diagnosis, and treatment planning with the primary purpose of enhancing the effectiveness of health services. Developing case conceptualisation skills is considered a core requirement for most health service professionals who specialise in mental health. Overall, research suggests that a therapist's ability to integrate client data successfully (case conceptualisation) is directly related to their cognitive developmental level (Rønnestad & Skovholt, 2003) and thus is often further developed through supervision.

DOI: 10.4324/9781003364207-13

Evidence-Based Practice, Spirituality, and Case Conceptualization

Evidence-based practice is about "attuning psychotherapy to the particulars of the individual according to the generalities of the research findings" (Norcross & Wampold, 2018). In addition to basic case conceptualisation from a CBT lens, before finalising a treatment plan, I prefer to first intellectually labour over the iconic question put forth by Paul (1969) which is "What treatment, by whom, is most effective for this individual with that specific problem, under which set of circumstances, and how does it come about?" (p. 44). Deconstructing this, there are at least four essential questions to answer in the case of conceptualisation. They are:

1 What treatment is most effective for this specific client?
2 What specific problem is the client seeking treatment for?
3 What are the circumstances?
4 How does the change come about?

In the initial session, one of the primary objectives for the CBT practitioner is to develop a case conceptualisation, also known as a case formulation. de Abreu Costa & Moreira-Almeida (2022) identified that at this stage, spiritual assessment is also important. However, to assume that all Muslims prefer an Islāmically integrated approach to therapy is an overgeneralisation. Likewise, to assume that a Muslim client who prefers an Islāmic approach does not also prefer a secular approach is also problematic. That is, the position taken by IMCBT is that the two are not mutually exclusive and can be seamlessly integrated. This position allows for a more flexible approach by the therapist in adapting to the multiple preferences and dynamics of the client.

Although existing spiritual assessments and the cultural formulation interview are quite useful to work across cultures, more is certainly needed to work effectively with diverse Muslims. Hence, psychologists who are acculturated to the diverse Islāmic ways of life, are familiar with cultural norms, and can straddle between Islāmic and secular rationales can be much more effective. Unfortunately, research on integrating spirituality in practice often lacks theoretical, ethical, and practical guidelines (Canda & Furman, 2010). Therefore, placing the onus on the individual practitioner to develop their own creative approaches or utilise the limited resources available in Islāmically modifying evidence-based practices at a deeper level.

In my practice, I prefer to take a parsimonious and metatheoretical approach to case conceptualisation beginning with the essentials of physical and psychological health and how they impact the client's social and occupational domains. Thus, by borrowing from the occupational therapy profession we can further enhance the assessment of the occupational domain, without compromising fidelity. It is also from here that the research on rituals, routines, roles, and spirituality is far more pronounced. This helps to understand the nature of the problem and inform the diagnosis. While doing so, we are also identifying patterns from the client's utterances and statements to understand how best to adapt the treatment approach while also better understanding the circumstances that need to be considered. The primary reason for this is that we cannot assume that CBT is the best treatment before meeting the client. Thus, when integrating spirituality for Muslims, the essentials of spiritual health and well-being are integrated with the essentials of physical and psychological health and well-being.

Furthermore, CBT and the bio-psycho-social model share a holistic approach to understanding and addressing human functioning and well-being. Both approaches emphasise the importance of considering interconnected biological, psychological, and social factors that influence health outcomes. They recognise the significance of cognitive processes, emotions, behaviours, and social context in shaping an individual's well-being. CBT focuses on modifying cognitive processes and behaviours while the bio-psycho-social model expands on this by incorporating social and environmental influences. Together, they offer a comprehensive understanding of human functioning and promote comprehensive care for individuals. Another way of infusing Islām into case conceptualisation is to connect the objectives of Islām to the objectives of psychology as previously discussed.

The As, BEES, and Cs of Health and Well-Being

The As of Spiritual Health and Well-Being

A comprehensive case conceptualisation that integrates Islāmic essentials can be quite meaningful and enhance the conceptualisation further. One way of doing so could be to use the As of spiritual health and well-being which I often incorporate with Muslim clients. Despite the differences between Muslims, ideologically or methodologically, three essentials can be agreed upon by all. They are the importance of the Islāmic creed (or *aqeedah*), good characteristics (*akhlaq*), and actions of the heart, tongue, and limbs (*aamaal al quloob, lisan, and jawarih*). Recall, dynamic bilingualism involves the fluid use of two languages, incorporating elements from both languages in communication or writing. In this case, I am using English letters to represent Arabic sounds, like substituting "A" for the Arabic letter "*Ayn*".

Aqeedah is an Arabic word that can be summarised as the five pillars of Islām and the six pillars of faith (although it goes much deeper than just the practices and basic beliefs). *Akhlaq* or characteristics are considered to be an essential Islāmic virtue and one of the most highly rewarded. The Prophet (ﷺ) said, "Nothing is heavier upon the scale of a believer on the Day of Resurrection than their good character" (al-Tirmidhī(e)). *Amaal* are actions that can be broken down into actions of the tongue, limbs, and heart.

The BEES of Physical Health

The BEES of physical health, consisting of breathing, eating, exercise, and sleep, are key components of maintaining good physical health. These factors are essential for survival and play a vital role in supporting overall well-being. Several interventions can focus on improving these areas that are often endorsed across most therapies, including CBT. Breathing exercises, such as diaphragmatic breathing and mindfulness-based breathing techniques, can enhance relaxation and reduce stress. Dietary interventions may involve promoting balanced eating habits, mindful eating, and nutritional education. Physical activity interventions can include creating exercise plans, encouraging regular movement, and providing guidance on appropriate exercises. Sleep hygiene practices, relaxation techniques, and addressing sleep disorders can help improve sleep quality.

CBT for insomnia (CBT-I) is an evidence-based intervention targeting sleep habits including scheduling issues, faulty thinking about sleep, and other factors that tend to perpetuate or aggravate challenges with sleep (Okajima, Komada, & Inoue, 2011). One often overlooked challenge that can be quickly addressed in therapy includes poor sleep hygiene practices (e.g. excessive caffeine use, irregular sleep schedules). These are considered to be major risk factors and serve as a deleterious course modifier. Thus, to increase the likelihood for positive therapeutic outcomes, focusing effort on psychoeducation and behavioural change with respect to sleep hygiene practices and other techniques is likely to show promise.

The Cs of Psychological Health and Well-Being

The Cs of psychological health and well-being, derived from self-determination theory (SDT), are connectedness (relatedness), choice (autonomy), and competence. SDT posits that these three basic psychological needs are essential for optimal motivation, development, and well-being (Deci & Ryan, 1985). This can be mapped onto three core aspects of the themes in Beck's cognitive theory on control, acceptance, and competence.

Connectedness refers to the need for meaningful and positive relationships with others, a sense of belonging, and social integration. It involves feeling connected, supported, and valued by family, friends, community, or larger social groups. When individuals experience connectedness, they feel understood, accepted, and emotionally supported. Connectedness is related to the Islāmic concept of *silah* or choice and refers to the need for autonomy and the ability to make decisions that align with one's own values, interests, and preferences. It involves having a sense of agency and control over one's actions and experiencing freedom in decision-making. It is connected to the Islāmic concept of intentions. Competence refers to the need to feel effective, capable, and competent in one's actions and pursuits. It involves developing and utilising one's skills, experiencing mastery, and achieving a sense of accomplishment. When individuals have opportunities to learn, grow, and demonstrate their abilities, it enhances their self-confidence, motivation, and well-being. It can be connected to the Islāmic concept of rewards.

Assessing Culture

Although there can be more intracultural differences than intercultural, it is important to not get bogged down with "paralysis by analysis" but rather, an appeal to a credible degree of closure. Thus, instead of trying to identify a comprehensive list of cultural adaptations, I will focus mainly on what other scholars have recommended in terms of basic strategies to enhance CBT's cultural responsiveness outlined by Hays (2009). In Hays, assessing the client and their family's needs is important. Thus, I usually replace the A in SMART goals with Agreed upon instead of Achievable, as I believe Achievable can be implied from the Realistic and Measurable elements of a SMART goal. Thus, I may ask, would this goal be agreeable to your mom, dad, spouse, and so on. The next recommendation in Hays and encouraged in Beck (2021) is culturally respectful behaviours. Cultural sensitivity is thus necessary but not sufficient for this criteria. Next is more specific to each client and that is identifying their strengths and supports they derive from their culture or faith. Finally, they add that validating the client's experiences with oppression is also important. This is something that has taken a much more important discourse in the field of psychology and will continue to be important.

11 Islāmic Life Values and the Qabool Alliance Model

In many of the religiously adapted CBT manuals, a section on encouraging clients to identify and work towards various life values is found. For example, in the RCBT manual, one of the core tools used is cultivating forgiveness, hope, gratitude, and generosity through daily religious practices. In this chapter, I highlight the virtue of *qabool* and explain how this life value can integrate a variety of other values while also serving as an ethical and practical framework along with a case example of how some aspects of it can be applied with a Muslim client using IMCBT.

Qabool Alliance Model: An Islāmically Integrated Evidence-Based Ethical and Practice Model

Acceptance in human psychology is a person's assent to the reality of a situation, recognising a process or condition without attempting to change it or protest it ("Acceptance," n.d.(b)). Thus, to define *qabool* as simply acceptance would lose its true essence. Nonetheless, *qabool*, a Qur'ânic Arabic word denoting acceptance, stands in stark contrast to rejection. The trilateral root word for *qabool* is Q-B-L (ق ب ل) and occurs 294 times in the Holy Qur'ân with 20 instances specifically related to acceptance (The Qur'ânic Arabic Corpus, 2022). Striving for acceptance of efforts is the ultimate objective of Muslims and is a spiritual endeavour that is enhanced through aspirational standards of ethics and behaviour (or being and doing). This principle was exemplified by Abraham (Peace Be Upon Him) and given as an honour to Mary (Peace Be Upon Her) and her Mother (Peace Be Upon Her).

After building the Kaabah, Abraham and his Son Ishmael (Peace Be Upon Them) made the following supplication:

- *And [mention] when Abraham was raising the foundations of the House and [with him] Ishmael, [saying], "Our Lord, accept [this] from us. Indeed You are the Hearing, the Knowing".*

(Al Baqarah, 2: 127)

DOI: 10.4324/9781003364207-14

As for Mary, the mother of Jesus (Peace Be Upon Them), as a child growing up in the care of Zachariah (Peace Be Upon Him), she was bestowed with *qabool* from Allāh the Almighty.

- *So her Lord accepted her with good acceptance and caused her to grow in a good manner.*

(Ali 'Imran, 3: 37)

Notwithstanding the many lessons and principles that can be derived from these two instances, *qabool* can be conceptualised as an outcome to strive for spiritually. *Qabool* can also be conceptualised as an ethical principle related to accepting the client as is, or in Rogerian terms, unconditional positive regard. Above all other principles, *Respect for the Dignity of Persons and Peoples* "is the most fundamental and universally found ethical principle across disciplines" (Canadian Psychological Association, 2017, Principle I, Values Statement). This principle consists of several standards often consistent across disciplines including but not limited to general respect, rights, non-discrimination, informed consent, privacy, and confidentiality. Violations of these standards carry a heavyweight in regulated professions.

However, how one achieves this outcome with their creator is a matter beyond the scope of this book. Rather, how *qabool* is achieved amongst people can be attributed to one's relationship with Allāh based on the following Hadīth.

> Abu Huraira reported: The Messenger of Allāh, peace and blessings be upon him, said, "When Allāh loves a servant, he calls Gabriel and he says: Verily, I love this person so you should love him. Then Gabriel loves him and makes an announcement in the heavens, saying: Allāh loves this person and you should love him. Thus, the dwellers of the heavens love him and he is honoured (with Qabool) on the earth".
>
> (Bukhârî (g))

If we engage in some *taddabur* or deep contemplation (and not *tafsir* or exegesis) of this Hadīth, we can see the association between having good *akhlaq* (characteristics) as one pathway to how one gets *qabool* amongst people. It could be one explanation to why we may just like someone before even meeting them. From a psychological perspective, this type of interpersonal attraction could be explained biologically, cognitively, affectively, socially, culturally, or some combination of all five (APA, n.d). Despite no consensus on the pathways or underlying mechanisms behind automatic attraction, from both a secular and Islāmic perspective, the proposition is that acceptance or *qabool* is a basic minimum attitude and state to strive for and is hypothesised to serve as an essential component of the therapeutic alliance.

Qabool Alliance Model

The Qabool Alliance Model can thus be viewed as an Islāmically integrated ethical and practice framework that can facilitate IMCBT. In practice, it includes three phases: (1) *sallam* (peace), (2) *taaruf* (understanding), and (3) *shura* (mutual consultation). The family resemblance between each stage can be explained with respect to common counselling phases and mapped onto evidence-based practices (i.e. rapport, assessment, and goal planning). The ethical framework is derived and operationalised from five authentic teachings of the Prophet Muhammad (ﷺ), four of which are related to positive attitudes, behaviours, and characteristics (collectively referred to as *akhlaq*) and one related to four negative behaviours conceptualised as symptoms of hypocrisy (*nifaq*). Thus, the ethical framework consists of two core principles (pro-*akhlaq* and anti-*nifaq*) and eight standards derived and operationalised from the five authentic prophetic teachings.

The scholar, Al-Khaleel Abu Muhammad Abdullah ibn Abu Zaid posited that all *akhlaq* can be derived from four *aHadīth* (prophetic traditions) and is used by imam An-Nawawi in his explanation of Sahih Muslim. These four *aHadīth* are the primary standards that form the basis of the *akhlaq* principle and can be explained in terms of actions (of the tongue and heart) and restraint.

Standard 1: Positive Communication and Restraint

(1) Whoever believes in Allāh and the Last Day, let him speak good or remain silent (Bukhârî (e)).

Standard 2: Empathy

(2) None of you will have faith until he loves for his brother what he loves for himself (Bukhârî (h)).

Standard 3: Focus on the Client and the Presenting Concern

(3) Verily, from the perfection of Islām is that a person leaves what does not concern him (al-Tirmidhī(f)).

Standard 4: Emotional Restraint

(4) Do not get angry (Bukhârî (i)).

The following Hadīth is where the four symptoms of hypocrisy are derived from and subsequently the anti-hypocrisy principles.

> Abdullah ibn Amr reported: The Messenger of Allāh, peace and blessings be upon him, said, "There are four signs that make someone a pure hypocrite and whoever has them has a characteristic of hypocrisy until he abandons it: when he speaks he lies, when he makes a covenant he is

treacherous, when he makes a promise he breaks it, and when he argues, he is wicked."

(Bukhârî (j))

Standard 5: Lying
Standard 6: Breaking a Promise
Standard 7: Breaking a Trust
Standard 8: Arguing Wickedly

The argument in this section is that violation of these standards is antithetical to *akhlaq* and characteristic of *nifaq*. Thus, it should be common knowledge that violating the principle of respect for the dignity of persons is a violation of Islāmic principles and thus would automatically violate any code of conduct in Islāmic institutions. In the interest of protecting the practitioner (from *nifaq*) and the guest (from harm), working from a clear and concise Islāmic ethical framework is necessary for *qabool* at both a spiritual and professional level.

Thus, at the most basic level, the practitioner demonstrating *akhlaq* constantly aspires and works towards developing the skills of managing their own emotions (do not get angry), considers the guest's needs above all others (love for them what you love for yourself), enquire about only pertinent information (leave what does not concern you), and utilises language that is supportive and non-judgemental (speak good or stay silent). This is also contrasted with four preventable behaviours related to *nifaq* (hypocrisy). These include different conceptualisations of lying to the guest, violating the therapeutic contract, reneging on promises, and arguing in a wicked manner (all directly related to respecting the dignity of persons as well as other ethical principles). In the following case, these core principles were used throughout the session in different ways. For example, the characteristics of hypocrisy were used to help her assess her public behaviour to challenge her dysfunctional thoughts. Thus, beyond simply encouraging clients to practise their life values, having a framework to bring them together can be quite promising.

The Case of Saleema

Early in the session after engaging in my typical approach, probing the guest to share what she would want to focus on, she quickly states she wants to talk about her anger. She then goes on to explain how irritated and bothered she becomes by small things. As she continues to discuss the many challenges, she gives a simple example that she considers to be shallow. This is where the opportunity to utilise a small possibly insignificant issue to her advantage arose. That is, invalidating can happen so easily, as discussed, so when the issue is minor, it reduces the likelihood of leading to a rupture or a period of poor relatedness. Furthermore, it's important to recognise that many small stressors can accumulate to seem like insurmountable stress. The objective of the session was thus threefold: to reduce immediate harm (in the form of over medicating and anger reduction), to challenge the dysfunctional thinking associated with the anger, and to identify what I call psycho-spiritual first-aid strategies for the guest to implement. Additionally, she explained that she recently started taking an extra half-tablet, which is helpful, though the side effects cause her to sleep too much. She mentioned she will speak to the physician about it. She states:

Saleema: For example, I was speaking to the internet company and she kept on offering me new deals and I couldn't take it. I know this is a simple issue but I get so angry and it's too much for me.

After allowing her ample time to express herself, I am listening not only for the narrative but also looking for blind spots. I explained to her how taking this as an example is a good idea, even if it is in her opinion minor it can help us uncover what's going on in the factory underneath. I began by focusing on providing psychoeducation on anger. Now, imagine how the session would have changed if I simply said "the Prophet (ﷺ) said, "don't get angry". Instead, I continued to explore her BEES, and C's, and reviewed the arguing with *Shaytan* concept.

Mahdi: What's the harshest word in your dialect to say be quiet – in mine, it's *Ikhras*, but I often say to myself, that's stupid shut up.
Saleema: hahaha. In mine, it's *sid thummak.*
Mahdi: Yes, say that and make it harsh. It's OK. Speak good or *sid thummak* (Shut your mouth).
Saleema: I was not like this, I am a calm and peaceful woman, why have I become like this.

This led to a dialogue around private and public lives which segued nicely into applying the *akhlak bidoon nifaq* (loosely translated into characteristics without hypocrisy) as an intervention.

At the time of this session, I had been writing about this topic and researching it heavily for developing it as an Islāmically integrated ethical framework. But this was the first time it was offered as an actual intervention, which led me to examine it deeper as a practice framework. I simply used the Hadīth on hypocrisy as an assessment tool and asked her to reflect on her behaviour in public one symptom at a time (lying, breaking trust, breaking promises, and arguing wickedly).

Mahdi: So you are not a hypocrite in public. Now let's look at the *akhlaq* part.
I reminded her of the Hadīth and she stated it.
Saleema: I know but it's so hard. But I want to master my anger.
Mahdi: Of course, if you can master it, you'd be like the *awliya* (saints), but you have to manage it first. But there's a phrase you mentioned

three times now and I let it slide, but I am going to challenge you on it. You said – it's too much for me. Is it really too much for you?

Commentary

One may be inclined to use the verse related to "Allāh does not test you beyond what you can bear", but this can be a type of toxic positivity or conversation killer. Instead, maintaining a focus on the irrational thought that often leads to avoidance (it's too hard, I am not competent enough and thus I won't try) is more meaningful while aiming to let the client invoke such verses or concepts on her own.

We continued to engage in Socratic dialogue and identified counter-examples to things that were once hard for her but she overcame. The focus was on challenging the negative self-talk related to the theme of incompetence.

Mahdi: The state before hopelessness is helplessness. What do you think happens to your body when you tell yourself I can't do it anymore? It must react.

Mahdi: So you can't say that anymore. You can say it's too much, it sucks, and swear as much as you like, but you can't say it's too much for me.

Saleema: (chuckling) OK, OK, I won't do that anymore. Sometimes, I make *dua* that Allāh helps me to stop thinking so much and to forget, and *subhanAllāh* it works.

Mahdi: It's such a blessing isn't it?

Saleema: Yes, I talk to myself so much.

Mahdi: That's the goal, to have you speak to yourself with more compassion and with evidence. Look at what happens when you allow those thoughts to take over, you start to think about things that don't even matter, like being sold up for the internet. So what, let her do her job, but I get it. Love for others what you love for yourself right? We love others to give us the benefit of the doubt. To have *husnul than* (positive and rational opinions).

Saleema: Yes, but it's very hard.

Mahdi: Of course. But sometimes we just have human moments, so it's OK that you get angry.

Saleema: (chuckles with a sigh of relief).

She then proceeds to compare herself to her friend which was another area that required some challenging.

Saleema: I have a friend who is so calm, I wish I was like her.

Mahdi: In public, but what about her private life. I'm sure she is wonderful, but you can't compare your private life to others' public behaviours. Remember, "leave what does not concern you".

Saleema: But I travelled with her.

Mahdi: And how were you when you travelled with her?

Saleema: I was fine, I was happy, and we had a really good time.

Mahdi: She probably thinks the same about you. But that's not the point, the point is there is an incongruence between your public and private life, and that's where we want to work on.

Saleema: Yes, I want a balance.

This was followed by a lengthy discussion around how exhausting it can be to apologise, how one moment of patience (*sabr*) can prevent a thousand moments of guilt (*nadm*). And how long the guilt should last.

As we were wrapping up the session, I summarised briefly what we discussed and then stated:

Mahdi: I know this all could sound *mithali* (ideal), but it works.

Saleema: Life is hard.

Mahdi: Certainly, but *La yukalifullahu* (Allāh does not test a person) (then intentionally paused) . . .

Saleema: (enthusiastically) *illa wus3aha* (except what it can bear), yes that's right. I can do it.

Mahdi: I know you can because you've done it before.

Saleema: Thank you, every time I speak to you I feel better and like I can manage it.

If an Islāmic concept is used too early, it can be one of those conversation killers that are counterproductive to therapy. But in this case, I felt it was appropriate as she filled in the rest. One indicator of success is how the client responds to the statement and whether they add anything to it. Furthermore, the goal is to have them state something like "that's right" rather than " you're right". This indicates that they have processed the information and accommodated it into their own beliefs. Furthermore, if after explaining an Islāmic teaching they begin to feel ashamed by saying something like "I should know this" or "I tell my friends that all the time", it's a good idea to use some immediacy to give the client back some agency. For example, I would often say something like "that's why we have each other, to remind ourselves we can't always be perfect, nor should we", followed by the verse in the Qur'ân on how reminders are beneficial to the believers.

12 Islāmically Modified Motivational Strategies and the Tawheed Taxonomy

Religion and spirituality constitute vital facets of cultural identity that, among various other elements detailed in this book, hold the potential to enhance positive therapeutic outcomes. Drawing a clear difference between the two can be challenging. However, in IMCBT, assessing Islāmic religiosity encompasses the visible actions or conduct undertaken by Muslim clients. Religiosity becomes evident through actions that symbolise the manifestation of faith, primarily observable and often, though not exclusively, obligatory (for instance, obligatory prayers in Islām, fasting during Ramadan, attending the mosque for Friday prayers). These actions are quantifiable and amenable to observation, making them conducive to establishing specific, measurable goals in collaboration with the client. However, Islāmic spirituality encompasses the personal valuation of practices and the subjective facets that clients express in terms of emotions and thoughts and delves into a deeper affiliation with religious practices or the inherent significance of these actions and can be highly dynamic and subjective. For instance, the act of prayer can be dissected into both quantitative and qualitative elements. Quantifying the frequency of prayer is straightforward, yet how does one ascertain the essence of a meaningful prayer experience? This nuanced enquiry delves into the subjective qualities of prayer engagement, capturing the depth of personal connection and intrinsic resonance that often elude quantification.

Religious Mustivation and Wantivation

Religion tends to emanate from external motivation or “Mustivation” (Vansteenkiste, 2013) stemming from obligation and external or internal pressure (such as “I must pray” or “I’m glad I completed the prayer”). However, spirituality emerges from autonomous motivation or “Wantivation” which is often more voluntary and pleasurable. Despite the obligatory nature of the five daily prayers, when accompanied by a sense of elation during or before prayer, like “I feel tranquil” or “I eagerly await prayer”, it indicates higher

DOI: 10.4324/9781003364207-15

levels of spirituality. Both exert influential motivational forces, with the latter representing a heightened level of personalisation and internalisation of behaviours. In simple terms, religion can be like doing tasks you have to do, and we can count those tasks. But spirituality is about how you feel inside when you do those things, and that's a bit harder to measure.

In this chapter, an analysis is made of a case example of a Muslim client who prematurely terminated with his therapist after a comment she made in terms of a clinical hypothesis that was considered to be evidence-based and consistent with her therapeutic approach. In other words, on the face of the record, she did not do anything intentionally wrong, was practising in accordance with her training and the standards of her profession, yet due to a cultural faux pas caused harm to her client which resulted in premature termination and a sense of bitterness in the client towards the field. In particular, the client stated during the session that he "must pray" which was responded with "maybe that is the problem". In this chapter, the motivational component of treatment is deconstructed and reframing "I must pray" to "I want to pray" is discussed in light of self-determination theory and the process of moving from external to internal motivation applied to the psychological, occupational, and spiritual domains of health and well-being.

This case study will be deconstructed and analysed providing the advantageous use of IMCBT in this case. Utilising the client's spiritual motivation will be deconstructed with the goal of helping the client to enhance both his mental and spiritual health with respect to the prayer. One objective that will be explained in detail will be the idea of reframing "I must pray" to "I want to pray". This objective will be discussed in light of self-determination theory and the process of moving from external to internal motivation applied to the psychological, occupational, and spiritual domains of health and well-being. Furthermore, it will be explained as signifying a shift from the Islāmic level of religiosity to the higher *iman* (faith) levels which, from a CBP lens, is associated with higher levels of pleasure and satisfaction with religious practices and thus increases their likelihood for sustainability. This process towards *Istiqama* or consistency is considered from an Islāmic perspective to be the fruits of faith.

Similarly, if a client believes that their fatigue, sleep disturbances, low mood, sadness, and loss of motivation are because they have stopped praying, then why not focus on the behaviour rather than the explanation? When people are suffering, they are more in need of our support than our speculations. Hence, for the counsellor, your initial role is not to force the client to believe in your worldview but to operate within their own. When the therapist said to Adam, maybe that is the problem, they had been operating on a core belief in their therapeutic approach. However, this would violate the client's certainty as theories and hypotheses are supposed to be subject to falsifiability. Hence, the use of the term "maybe". But this is not what was heard by the client. Rather, the client interpreted this statement to mean, "your rigid thinking about your prayer is causing this distress and we should talk about that". Had the therapist introduced exposure and response prevention, that is, having the client not go to pray and addressing the negative emotional feelings through mindfulness and relaxation therapy, it would be evidence-based, but from the client's perspective, torturous and offensive. If a therapist does not understand that for Adam, prayer is a fundamental need, depriving him of this basic need would be akin to someone who is thirsty and says, "I have to drink water" and the response is "maybe that is the problem".

In cultural assessments, it is important to not only understand what is important for clients but also assess the weight of such importance. For Adam, prayer is ranked at the top of his list, even above eating and sleeping. He has not been eating or sleeping well and rarely exercises. These are, in fact, the problems that should be focused on first. This is another example of the difference between theory and practice. In this specific instance, Adam was indeed obsessing on his need to pray with a resulting compulsion to stand up. Thus, his fidgeting was a natural bodily reaction as a result. The therapist, with good intentions and perhaps based on solid psychological evidence, made an error in judgement. Of course, it is very likely that this was the proverbial "straw that broke the camel's back", and the termination was a result of a series of ruptures in the relationship (or multiple periods of non-relatedness), but I believe the lessons learned can be many. As a corrective, the next case provides a detailed account of how one could approach the issue of both challenging the rigid thinking and shifting one's motivation from external to internal or shifting from "mustivation to wantivation" with respect to spiritual practices.

The Case of Saleh

Saleh is a 12-year-old Muslim boy who has started homeschooling last year and has been referred to me by his parents to focus on his motivation. I requested to have a brief consult with the parents as I am quite familiar with the dynamics of the *Tahfeez* programme (a Qur'ân memorisation school that has become a newer phenomenon in the West) and want to ensure that parents are comfortable with my approach; especially since I will likely challenge some commonly held beliefs to replace them with more optimised ones from an Islāmic perspective. After discussing the parents' concerns, although they were initially mainly concerned about his video game use, and his emotional reactions while playing video games, I explored this issue with them from a model for managing addictions that I use.

Basically, I explain that the prohibition of ingesting intoxicants came in three phases (explain these phases and the verses associated). Then I explain, it is important to assess if he sees the harm in excessive video game use, and they acknowledge that he does but cannot be certain. I then queried, does it interfere with important activities, like the prayer, they said no it does not. At this point, they did not seem to feel the video games were the real problem, and so after explaining how video games are so powerful, I asked,

Mahdi: Wouldn't it be amazing if he loved Prayer as much as he loves video games? But aren't we all on that same journey?

They seemed to get it, so I asked them about the positive things they like about their son, and they are very proud of him, acknowledging that they don't express that enough because they have such high expectations for him. Furthermore, they explained that they don't really see him as having any major disorders, but they want to prevent this issue from getting worse as he seems to be going through puberty, and they are concerned.

I continue to discuss with them motivation and explain intrinsic motivation and personality development from a self-determination theory and connect it to the Islāmic perspective. I also introduce the Tawheed taxonomy as a stage model of intrinsic motivation and spiritual development.

Commentary

Often, the goals of Islāmic interventions are to help individuals establish a deep connection with Allāh, align their lives with Islāmic principles, and find emotional, psychological, and spiritual well-being through the application of faith. Combining psychological interventions with Islāmic teachings provides a holistic framework for addressing various mental health and personal growth issues. However, limited frameworks exist to provide a comprehensive account of Islāmic spirituality development. Thus, in this session, I utilised a framework that I have been developing for this specific purpose called the Tawheed taxonomy.

Shaykh Hafiz al-Hukmi, in his poem Sullam al-Wusul, emphasises seven conditions associated with the affirmation of the *Shahadah* or the testimony of faith in the Oneness of Allāh and the Prophet Muhammad as his Messenger (ﷺ) which underpins Islāmic belief. They are:

1 Knowledge: علم (*ʿilm*)
2 Certainty: يقين (*yaqīn*)
3 Acceptance: قبول (*qabūl*)
4 Submission: إنقياد (*inqiyād*)
5 Truthfulness: صدق (*ṣidq*)
6 Sincerity: إخلاص (*ikhlāṣ*)
7 Love: محبة (*muḥabbah*)

When looked at as a stage model, this taxonomy can be quite meaningful in therapy. They appreciate the stages and agree with the rationale. I then explain that.

Mahdi: It appears your son has strong knowledge and certainty, as well as *qabool* (acceptance), and *inqiyad* (submission). And for his age that is amazing. But what I hear you saying is that you know he can be better, and perhaps that is the main reason you are here and not because there is any serious problem.

The parents agree, and it is likely that this alleviated their initial worries as the issue was reframed from a problem-centred one to a solution-focused one.

Mahdi: Then, what we would need to work on is his truthfulness (to himself), sincerity, and eventually love.

The parents agree this is a feasible model and are grateful. I also introduce the concept of eventually working towards building a network of support for their son by utilising more Islāmic mentors and coaches. Since they are active in the Muslim community and have been involved with programmes in the past, they see this as a feasible plan and agree to begin looking. The following dialogue is one that I find often occurs with parents and also demonstrates that despite cultural barriers, when trust is established, many are quite likely to forego their apprehensions about losing control.

Mahdi: Before we do anything, we need to make sure that he is on board.
Parent: He will be.
Mahdi: I am confident of that too, but still, deeds are by intentions, and we need him to have the right intention.
Parent: Yes yes, Ok, I will bring him.
Mahdi: If you trust me, then trust my process, I may need to kick you out of the room, so do not be offended.
Mahdi: Of course not, please do that, I really appreciate it.

Now that I have the parents on board with my process, I can be genuine and present for Saleh making his goals a priority without any pressure from the parents. This is not to say that the parents do not still have authority over my work with him, as he is a minor, rather they have symbolically transferred their authority to me.

The First Session

Mahdi: How do you feel about the prayer now?
Saleh: I feel forced to pray (his head is down and not making eye contact, and I can sense he feels ashamed).

Mahdi: Forced?

Saleh: Like, I'm going to still pray, but I don't really . . . well . . . I am not "intrinsically motivated".

Mahdi: Oh you mean you feel like you have to do it for some reason.

Saleh: Yeah.

Mahdi: Like you are motivated but because you have to do it.

Saleh: Uh huh.

Mahdi: Guess what, that's how everybody feels, and we spend our lives trying to achieve what the Prophet ﷺ had "coolness of my eyes" (Hadīth explained in commentary). It's his favourite thing.

Saleh: (as his face lights up and he begins to make more eye contact as though burden has been lifted) Really?

Mahdi: (Explain the Hadīth where the Prophet says to Bilal, get up and ease us with it, referring to the prayer).

Mahdi: Imagine how you feel when you play your favourite video game.

Saleh: Ahh yeah I get it –

Mahdi: Would that be something you would want to have for the prayer?

Saleh: Oh yeaah definitely.

Mahdi: This is proof that it is not forced, because it's not externally controlled but rather internal. For example, so, even if you miss *fajr* prayer, what do you do?

Saleh: I make it up.

Mahdi: That's *Qadda* (making up the prayer). So you do the right thing when you make a mistake. Does anyone have to remind you?

Saleh: Not really, I'll do it myself.

Mahdi: So it sounds like you are going to do it if you like it or not?

Saleh: Yeah pretty much.

Mahdi: That's called ISLĀM.

Saleh: Huh?

Mahdi: Yeah, submission, and usually because we fear punishment.

Saleh: Yeah, is that bad or good?

Mahdi: We don't look at it that way, it's more of a phase you are in. You are either not motivated, externally motivated, or internally motivated. But internally motivated is not always fun, it can be pressure.

Saleh: OK (not really understanding but intrigued).

Mahdi: If it were externally controlled, when no one is around, you wouldn't do it. But, the internal pressure usually starts with fear of punishment, and then we work towards the promise of the reward. But fear of punishment is not sustainable.

Saleh: I see, so I would start wanting to do it to get into Jannah.

Mahdi: Exactly.

Saleh: Sort of like my memorisation of the Qur'ân, it's not always enjoyable but I do it.

Mahdi: Exactly, let's explore that deeper.

I learn that he has been able to memorise on his own on a daily basis and often enjoys it but lately has been feeling a little less motivated. I normalise this feeling once again and explain the difference between mustivation and wantivation.

Mahdi: You know, this is how we all feel as well about work, it's not always fun, but we do it, and there are a lot of great benefits.
Saleh: Yeah I agree.
Mahdi: It's also an important milestone for you as you become a man.
Saleh: What do you mean?
Mahdi: (I can notice he is likely reluctant to discuss puberty so I do not continue with that line of discussion but instead remain focused on motivation) I mean, becoming a man often comes with more responsibilities without the reward. It can't always be fun anymore.
Saleh: Ahh, yeah. I see.
Mahdi: But with Islāmic activities, it's a little different, this is expected. You know that in Islām, "*Al-iman yazeed wa yankus*" (Faith increases and decreases).
Saleh: Yeah, I learned that from one of my *shyookh.*
Mahdi: What does that mean to you?

He provides an accurate account of the meaning behind it which is another way of assessing his knowledge to more properly adapt to his stage of knowledge in order not to be too simplistic or complex. I then explain a Hadīth related to faith increasing and decreasing and connect this to motivation and having a basic baseline to not go under. We continue to discuss his normal routines and habits, and roles, and rituals to shift to establishing the specific tasks to achieve the goals. I also discover that at times, he may get distracted and pray close to the end of the allotted time. It appears that given his routines, time management may need to be a goal to work on. One outcome of this would be to avoid the biological response of feeling pressured, and I explain how the brain works under stress. I also sneak in a line saying that "especially when young people go through puberty this tends to be more sensitive". But I can see he is still embarrassed and not ready to open up about it, so I quickly move into the next point on basic relaxation strategies.

Close to the end of the session, as we summarised what we discussed and I checked in to see if there were any cognitive shifts, I explained that there are three things he can do right away. These prescriptive points would not normally be done with adults as I would normally ask them what they plan on doing this week and work from that angle. However, with youth, especially in cases where they are just beginning therapy, prescriptive plans can be quite beneficial.

Mahdi: As for connectedness, I want you to pray in congregation more. I would also like to connect you to some older Muslims who can be like your Ansar.

Saleh: Hahaha, my Ansar?!

Mahdi: Yeah! The Prophet Muhammad ﷺ and his closest companions amongst the Muhajireen made such a strong connection with the Ansar, and now look.

Saleh: Yeah that would be awesome.

Mahdi: But it has to be your choice, your intention, because if they think you are forced to do it, or don't want to be there, it won't work.

Saleh: I understand. Yes, I definitely would love that.

Mahdi: Speaking of *Niyyah* (intentions), if deeds are by intentions and what you intend to do you get rewarded for, I would like you to think of the next prayer in a different way by starting with your intention seeking the reward.

Saleh: OK.

Mahdi: So, re-read what you probably read many times about the benefits and rewards of prayer. Only this time, I want you to imagine that you will 100% certainly get those rewards because the promise of Allāh is always true. Can you do that for me?

Saleh: Yeah, I can do that.

Mahdi: Excellent. I am very excited to see you achieve your goal, and I hope this was not as bad as you thought it would be.

Saleh: No, no, no, I really liked it. *JazakAllāh u Khayr*.

After meeting the boy, my conceptualisation is the following. The parents are quite supportive but it appears they will need more support for him, especially for his Islāmic development and transition through puberty. His parents are very proud of his accomplishments and manners, but lately he has been getting irritated more quickly and appears to be in a low mood. There is no apparent social or occupational dysfunction, and although most of his symptoms can be normalised, he nonetheless would be better diagnosed using the V-Code in the DSM 5 – religious/spiritual problem. In this case, the objective of therapy was to enhance internal motivation. The approach taken is IMCBT utilising stages of problem-solving therapy to establish a long-term plan that consists of daily activities and routines to enhance his sense of competence, autonomy, and relatedness drawing from self-determination theory. Helping him to differentiate between control and pressure, by reminding himself that "you are doing all this because you want to do it, even if sometimes you have to do it, so your intention is in the right place".

Knowledge Is Necessary But Not Sufficient

Although knowledge is important, it is not the only factor in facilitating change; motivation needs to be taken into account. A significant theory in organisational psychology is the expectancy theory (Vroom, 1964), which includes three key components: valence, instrumentality, and expectancy.

Valence refers to the value a person places on a particular outcome or reward. It assesses whether the expected outcome is desirable or not. Instrumentality examines the belief that performing a certain action will lead to the desired outcome. It is about understanding the link between effort and outcome. Expectancy is about the belief that the effort invested will actually lead to the desired performance. Together, these components interact to influence an individual's motivation to perform a task or exhibit a particular behaviour. If any of these factors are low, it can diminish motivation and hinder behaviour change.

13 Islāmically Modified Cognitive Interventions

Highlighting the *Dua* Intervention

In approaches that are trans-diagnostic or solution-focused and do not necessarily address clinical symptoms that are indicative of a serious mental health disorder, the consequences are arguably less severe. For example, in culturally adapted interventions, the integration can be shallow and includes changing only the language while keeping everything else the same. A simple rendition of this would be to replace the Miracle question from solution-focused brief therapy with the *dua* (or supplication) question. That is, the miracle question is often used to elicit from the client what changes they hope to see by asking something akin to "if you went to sleep tonight and a miracle occurred and all of your problems went away, how would you know? What would you observe?" I have used this in sessions before by stating, "if you made dua for your problem to go away, and it was answered, how would you know? What would you see that proves this to you?" That is, the modification was based on content alone which would be considered a shallow modification.

The Case of Mr Ahmad

Ahmad is a 52-year-old married Arab male who has been working as a cab driver for 20 years. He came to Canada as an immigrant from Lebanon and has been leading a productive life. He values being independent and not in need of anyone and thus seeing a psychologist was something he never thought he would do. He was involved in a motor vehicle accident and was referred for psychological services by his physician. He has been on a leave of absence from work due to injuries sustained in the accident and has recently returned to work.

Initially, Ahmad dismissed the need to see a psychologist as he felt it was not important. However, after returning to work on the first day, he felt extremely overwhelmed and frustrated. During our intake, he reports that on his way home, he kept ruminating on the argument he had with his wife before he left the house. On his way home, all he could think about was how upset he was with his wife. He explains that he could feel his rage building up, and no matter how hard he tried to suppress such thoughts, he was unsuccessful. He tried some basic Islāmic coping strategies, but they were not

DOI: 10.4324/9781003364207-16

successful. As we explored these thoughts, there was no need to challenge them as he agreed they were irrational. This led to exploring his thoughts from an Islāmic lens. He stated that he felt that these thoughts were more of a type of *waswasa* or whispers from the devil. Using his worldview as the foundation, the intervention went something like this:

Mahdi: So you have these thoughts and you keep arguing with your spouse in your mind and it keeps going back and forth?
Ahmad: Yes! Exactly!
Mahdi: But who are you really arguing with?
Ahmad: . . .
Mahdi: This internal arguing doesn't seem to make you feel any better does it?
Ahmad: Not at all.
Mahdi: Maybe you are arguing with your *shaytan* (devil).
Ahmad: Yeah. I never looked at it like that.
Mahdi: What if you tried making *dua* for her?
Ahmad: (a reluctant) OK . . . (requiring an explanation of the rationale).
Mahdi: The reason I say that is if you make *dua* for her, an angel will make *dua* for you, and when the angels show up, the devils disappear.
Ahmad: Haha, you are right.
Mahdi: So if that's the case, what else do we know about *shayateen* (devils) and how to block them.
Adam: *Istiaathah. Authoobillahi minal shaytan al rajeem* (I seek refuge in Allāh from the accursed satan).
Mahdi: Excellent, so what about entering the house and saying *sallam*.

Commentary

I was referencing an authentic Hadīth that Ahmad is familiar with. The Hadīth states:

> There is no Muslim who prays for his brother in his absence, but the angel will say: And you will have something similar.
>
> Muslim (f))

Whereas *istiaathah* (seeking refuge in Allāh from the whispers of the devils) is a cognitive stopping intervention, in this case, the issue was interpersonal and thus extending different interventions to focus on managing thoughts about his wife that lead to negative emotions and behaviours; especially upon entering the home as this will facilitate prevention.

Mahdi: When you think about your wife, is it possible that you are focusing only on the negative things and ignoring the positives?

Ahmad: Yeah I know I shouldn't do that. But I don't know, I just can't seem to help it, she makes me so angry.

Mahdi: OK, so I'd like you to experiment with something today. What I would like you to do is to put yourself into a *Shukr* (gratitude) mind-set. I would like you to instead of thinking about all the problems, think about the things you are truly grateful for that your wife does.

I would go on to explain a Qur'ânic theory, which is "if you are grateful, I will increase it" which is derived from the verse

- *And ʿrememberʾ when your Lord proclaimed, "If you are grateful, I will certainly give you more".*

(Ibrahim (Abraham) 14:7)

What we were able to focus on was helping him manage the cognitive error commonly known as filtering. The idea behind this distortion is that it leads to ignoring positive aspects related to the client's life and focusing only on the negatives. As we discussed this thinking error in more detail, the purpose was to help the client realise how they tend to trap themselves in dwelling on only the negative aspects of their situation and filter out all the positives.

Throughout the course of therapy with Ahmad, several cognitive distortions were addressed not just in relation to his wife. I had explained the elastic band technique and also used this as a metaphor for the stressors in his life. I had also provided him with an elastic band and explained the rationale on why a snap of the wrist can help to stop his ruminations for a brief moment.

Mahdi: You mentioned that your thoughts often feel like they're racing, and it's challenging to manage them. Can you tell me more about what happens when these thoughts start to overwhelm you?

Ahmad: It's like I start with a small thought, but then it just keeps growing and taking over everything.

Mahdi: It sounds like these thoughts become more intense and intrusive as they progress. This is where the elastic band comes in, snapping it against your wrist is the first step to interrupt these overwhelming thoughts.

Ahmad: Yeah, I do that, but the thoughts keep coming back.

Mahdi: Remember, it's a tool to help you regain control. The next step after using the elastic band is redirecting your thinking. This involves shifting your focus away from those intrusive thoughts and engaging in problem-solving techniques. But often what happens is we start by trying to problem-solve the past.

Ahmad: What do you mean?

Mahdi: Have you heard the Hadīth about: "Iyyakum wal law"? (Beware of Why).

Ahmad: Yes, I have. It is the worst of lies.
Mahdi: And it opens up doors to more irrational thoughts, "if only, I did this, things would be different".
Ahmad: Yes, I think I do that all the time.

Although CBT allows for such a technically eclectic approach, when addressing intrusive thoughts with Muslims, shallow approaches are not always useful, and thus deeper integration can be more advantageous than conventional approaches. For example, often, the etymology of intrusive thoughts attributed to demon possessions (*jin*) or whispers from the devil are indeed mental health challenges (Tanhan & Young, 2022). However, intrusive thoughts, even if conceptualised by the client as *jin* or devils, can still be treated from a deeper modification using the IMCBT approach. The cautionary note here is that if the client feels their worldview is being rejected or ridiculed, it can cause irreparable damage to the relationship. Thus, taking an IMCBT approach is warranted.

14 Tailoring Islāmically Modified Coping Strategies

Advanced Islāmically Modified Cognitive Behavioural Therapy

In Husain & Hodge's (2016) study, the authors discuss how CBT can be enhanced when working with devout Muslims by modifying traditional CBT self-statements to align with Islāmic values. The values that underpin Western counselling practices are compared with those of Islām, and areas of differing value emphasis are identified. That is, they explain that familiarity with Islāmic teachings and beliefs is essential for practitioners working with Muslims. Islām emphasises community, spirituality, and interdependence rather than individualism and secularism. Some Muslims may be uncomfortable with traditional CBT self-statements, as they tend to reinforce enlightenment or secular Euro-Western individualistic values. However, both Islām and the Enlightenment narrative acknowledge the importance of cognitive restructuring for mental health, but the value system conveyed through this process may differ. Understanding these differences can help to implement culturally appropriate interventions for Muslim clients.

As an alternative, Husain & Hodge (2016) put forth a process of constructing Islāmically modified CBT statements based on a previous study by Hodge and Nadir (2008). This three-step process includes:

1. Unpacking the European Enlightenment values embedded in the CBT self-statements used to convey the therapeutic concept.
2. Evaluating the basic concept to ensure it aligns with Islāmic values cherished by the client.
3. Repackaging the concept in Islāmic values that resonate with the client's belief system.

By doing so, the repackaged statement is likely to activate more transformative mechanisms. For example, they identify the concept, align it with Islāmic values, then repackage it into a self-statement.

> Misfortunes and blessings are from Allāh. Misfortunes are not terrible or awful, but rather a test. Although adversities may be unpleasant, we can

DOI: 10.4324/9781003364207-17

withstand them. Allāh tells us that He will not test us beyond what we can bear. By reminding ourselves of Allāh's goodness, and engaging in regular dua (informal prayer), we can cope with life's challenges.

(Hodge & Nadir, 2008, p. 37)

Their analysis is that the new statement not only integrates the client's worldview but also provides a different rationale for tolerating frustration; namely, that it is a test and that it will never be something they cannot bear thus reinforcing hope through challenging the dysfunctional thought that they cannot bear. This is also connected to perseverance or *sabr* and the action of *dua* or supplications.

Positive and Negative Religious Coping

In Bowland et al. (2012), their manualised RCBT aimed to help clients utilise or reevaluate their religious coping strategies in the context of trauma. Similar to other manuals, through psychoeducation, alternative interpretations, and the promotion of positive coping, clients were supported in using their spirituality as a source of strength and resilience during difficult times. However, what I find to be unique about this manual is the emphasis on negative religious coping strategies. When authors note that Islām influences every aspect of a Muslim's life, including how to behave during crisis and challenges, addressing emotional needs is part of it. What you will find if you dig deeper into the life of Muhammad PBUH is a profound framework for empathy and love for humanity. What you will not find is toxic positivity.

For some clients, embracing the belief that a problem or adversity may ultimately be good for them can be transformative. They may find solace in the understanding that hardships have a purpose and can lead to personal growth, character development, or spiritual elevation. This perspective can empower individuals to reframe their challenges as opportunities for learning, self-improvement, and drawing closer to Allāh (Husain & Hodge (2016). However, as therapists, we need to be able to recognise the difference between functional and dysfunctional self-statements.

Mr Alim

One of my clients, Mr Alim, would engage in positive self-statements that on the surface would seem like they were facilitating coping, but in fact, they were suppressing his emotional expression. For example, after discussing his deteriorating physical and mental health condition, he would say "But others have it way worse". Instead of agreeing with him, I would say "sure, but that doesn't make your problem any less severe". I found these types of responses (ones that return the focus back on him) to be quite validating and assisted greatly in moving the dialogue forward.

This process of him sharing his distress and quickly providing an ideal, often cliche, self-statement led me to more deeply examine his social support network and help-seeking attitudes. I did this because my hypothesis was that the style of support he receives is likely in the form of toxic positivity. My hypothesis was confirmed as he explained how he grew up in a rough neighbourhood and that emotional support was absent from his life. To which he quickly would say, "But that's just the way it is, I'm not complaining". The "thank God for the good and the bad" approach was quite meaningful in this case. I would ask, which do you want to focus on today, and he would usually respond "the Khayr (the good) is always the good". But quickly he would then begin speaking about his challenges. I maintained a CBT conceptualisation of his problem and worked towards extending his Islāmic coping strategies with different more relevant and facilitative self-statements. However, instead of just telling him, we would explore these together.

Mr Alim was suffering from severe depression associated with chronic pain and disability. Since he has been getting very angry lately, he has been feeling that he was not living in accordance with his values. Being a well-respected and active member in the community, he was not able to attend the mosque as often as he would like, and when he did, he felt embarrassed to sit on the chair.

The coping resources that seemed to be more conducive to allowing him to feel validated while also processing emotions were ones that focused on alternative ways of describing the nature of life and shifting to our role in this life accompanied with specific actions that can be taken. For example, two integrated concepts can be used. The first, where we come from and where we are going; the second, what we should do before we leave. For example, in the same verse often used to support the "life is a test" theme, using the verse that follows can facilitate a deeper dialogue. The verses are:

- *We shall certainly test you by afflicting you with fear, hunger, loss of properties and lives and fruits. Give glad tidings, then, to those who remain patient.*

  (Al Baqrah (The Cow) 2:155)

- *Those who when any affliction smites them, they say: "Verily, we belong to Allāh, and it is to Him that we are destined to return".*

  (Al Baqrah (the Cow) 2:156)

Thus, the concept that we belong to Allāh, and we will return to Allāh, can open up the dialogue on specific actions that need to be taken. For example, this Hadīth can also be used to facilitate this process and the idea that we cannot control what the future brings, but we can focus on the here and now.

> Narrated by Anas: A man asked the Prophet about the Hour (i.e. Day of Judgment) saying, "When will the Hour be?" The Prophet said, "What

> have you prepared for it?" The man said, "Nothing, except that I love Allāh and His Apostle". The Prophet said, "You will be with those whom you love". We had never been so glad as we were on hearing that saying of the Prophet (i.e., "You will be with those whom you love"). Therefore, I love the Prophet, Abu Bakr and "Umar, and I hope that I will be with them because of my love for them though my deeds are not similar to theirs".
>
> (Bukhârî (k))

Thus, being more creative in utilising multiple approaches to the "life is a test" theme is strongly encouraged. For some, being more creative can be quite meaningful. In several cases, especially younger clients, I would use humour to facilitate this.

When "Life Is a Test" Goes Wrong: The Case of Mariam

On the other hand, for certain individuals, this theme may inadvertently be interpreted in a more negative light; one of a toxic positivity nature. Toxic positivity occurs when individuals deny or suppress negative emotions, dismissing them as unimportant or invalid. In this context, interpreting every problem or hardship as inherently good can invalidate the genuine pain, struggles, and emotional difficulties experienced. It can also create an unrealistic expectation to constantly maintain a positive outlook and deny the human experience of suffering. For Maryam, this was quite apparent early on.

The Case of Mariam

Although this is perhaps one of the cases that I have integrated a wealth of Islāmic interventions, I will mention only one instance and leave the rest for another publication. I had encouraged her to begin journalling early on and welcomed her to send me whatever she likes in an email. Furthermore, she chose to record all of the sessions, and thus she would re-listen to them. She notes in one of her emails (copied and pasted as is with her permission but I changed the Arabic text into English transliteration):

Mariam: I tried to listen to most of the sessions we did last year, and wow, I am in awe.

I do know that the progression I made is fantastic. However, there are things I haven't even noticed I became better at like accepting praise and people speaking highly of me. That's huge!

I trained myself to *ahsanul than bilnaas* (Have *husnul than* or positive opinions of people) that people are not pitying me and not to insult their intelligence.

She then references a Hadīth I shared with her about praise by stating a few words. The full Hadīth is

> Abu Dharr reported: It was said to the Messenger of Allāh, peace and blessings be upon him, "What do you think of a man who does good deeds and people praise him?" The Prophet said, "They are early glad tidings for a believer".
>
> (Muslim (g))

It is important to note that, often, Muslims tend to view praise from a different perspective based on this Hadīth.

> It was narrated that Mu'awiyah said: "I heard the Messenger of Allāh (PBUH) say: 'Beware of praising one another, for it is slaughtering (one another)'".
>
> (Ibn Mājah (c))

This is another essential reason why scholarly opinions are needed when utilising Hadīth. This Hadīth in particular is often referring to empty and false praise rather than genuine praise for good deeds.

In a different email thread she references the "life is a test" motif that often gets mentioned. She begins the email with:

Mariam: I want to thank you for making me focus on the positive things going on in my life. I'm back to singing, dancing, and getting excited over little things again after experiencing the worst thoughts the last couple of days.

She then goes on to explain the results of her *taddabur* or deep reflection on Qur'ânic verses

Mariam: I was always frustrated because of this *ayah* (written in Arabic). We will certainly test you with a touch of fear and famine and loss of property, life, and crops. Give good news to those who patiently endure. Until these came to my awareness

- *Whoever does righteousness, whether male or female, while he is a believer – We will surely cause him to live a good life, and We will surely give them their reward [in the Hereafter] according to the best of what they used to do.*

  (Al Naml (The Bee) 16:97)

- *And what you have is an enjoyment of worldly life. But what is with Allāh is better and more lasting for those who have believed and upon their Lord rely.*

  (Al Qasas (The Stories), 28:60)

Commentary

The verse that triggered her frustration is the same one that is often repeated to invoke the "Life is a Test" coping strategy. The other verses she utilised go far beyond the idea that life is a test and introduce deeper concepts such as "the good life" (which she underlined), being rewarded for good deeds in this life and the next, and in the third verse she quoted, it provides perhaps a better appreciation for the limitations of this world and the temporary nature of distress. She would go on to say:

Mariam: So whenever I'm down that I don't have something specially "love", I ask Allāh "Oh God, compensate me and provide for me from what is enduring" (translated from Arabic).

Clinical Application

This client certainly had the knowledge as she is quite intelligent and well-versed in Islāmic principles. Furthermore, she did not suffer from crippling doubt but rather had both *yaqeen* and *qabool*. It is important to note that internal struggle is quite real, and we need to be careful not to assume the client must be ideal at all times; this would violate an essential Islāmic principle that *iman* (faith) increases and decreases, and sin is inevitable. Furthermore, it can assist with supporting the client to accept a problem rather than remain in denial. One client, who was highly religious, had no problem visiting me but tended to struggle to accept his mental health challenge. The statement that changed things around was likely this one.

Mahdi: Isn't it better to accept that you have a problem and expect the reward from Allāh for your patience, than to deny you have a problem and be punished for your lack of patience.

By drawing on Islāmic principles rather than CBT ones, RCBT can be enhanced and achieve the objectives of both fields when the coping strategy is either enhanced or replaced with a problem-solving strategy. For example, when one commits a sin, it can activate a highly rewarded act of repentance or *tawbah*. Drawing on the principles and processes of *tawbah*, a treatment plan can be developed. Furthermore, when discussing the issue of restorative justice, teaching clients about the ingredients of an effective apology can be quite effective.

Dual-Domain Expertise

Bowland et al. (2012) raise an important point which can be looked at as a recommendation for further research. They explain that all of the facilitators carrying out the RCBT had training in theology and pastoral care. Thus, they could be viewed as possessing traits of dual-domain expertise. Thus, they query whether or not this specialised training in theology and pastoral care could be a factor and thus be required as a prerequisite. This is perhaps much more relevant when negative styles of religious coping arise. At times, the negative religious coping style may be the one that needs challenging and replacement. But this could be a slippery slope for someone who is untrained, holds negative biases towards religion, or has no systematic method of providing the client with a better alternative within the boundaries of their worldview.

15 Conclusion

IMCBT and the Global Landscape of Mental Health

Advice is saying the right things, whereas counselling is responding to the right things. The concept that drives change isn't solely knowledge or skills but rather the presence of motivation and a conducive environment to put them into practice. Thus, giving advice, or saying the right things, despite being accurate, may not lead to the change required. If that were the case, then all we would need is education, and all of our problems would go away. Rather, we can draw on psychological theories to further understand how using Islāmic teachings can be more effective.

How change comes about or, the mechanism of change behind therapies can be categorised under three main types of factors that facilitate positive therapeutic outcomes: specific, common, and extra-therapeutic factors. For CBT, specific factors are primary mechanisms for change as identified in the theoretical underpinning. This is where breaking down CBT into its essential components allows us to see how Islāmic modifications can maintain their fidelity to these specific factors. The second type, common factors, are aspects of treatment that are common to all therapies. Although I often utilise CBT in my practice, my general approach to therapy is more metatheoretical and can be seen as being culturally adapted and localised evidence-based practices (e.g. recall the CARE in the CHAIR model in the introduction). When working with Muslims, this often includes innovative interventions that are more advantageous than conventional ones but can still be traced back to what psychological research supports. The third are extra-therapeutic factors or factors that influence outcomes outside of the treatment context. Thus, understanding the lived reality of Muslims is important; especially when treatment works best when the skills learned in therapy can be applied in the real world. However, to make any generalisations is to assume some degree of homogeneity, which you are likely not to find amongst the billion Muslims spanning the world today.

As the years go by, I am constantly reminded of how important it is for many of my Muslim clients/guests to recognise the infusion of Islāmic principles into every aspect of the counselling process. This extends beyond just the therapy and is embedded within the organisational culture, training,

DOI: 10.4324/9781003364207-18

supervision, and developing models and interventions to be, what I hope is, knowledge that benefits readers like yourself. For example, the reason I call my clients guests has everything to do with our hospitality culture. Thus, whether we call them guests, clients, or patients is irrelevant when compared to how we treat them. That is, everyone must (not should) be treated with a high level of hospitality and respect. The difference between hospitality as a culture and hospitality as a value is that as a culture, it permeates everything we do. Thus, hospitality is the guest's right, not a privilege. Imagine what it would be like to visit a health professional's clinic and to feel like you are the guest of honour. Would that impact how often you would get a routine check-up? Compare that to waiting for hours and being greeted with a long form to fill out.

What may very well be the underlying principles of success for my practice has to do with a hospitality culture in addition to the guiding principles that IMCBT is built on. For example, dynamic bilingualism. Although being able to communicate verbally and non-verbally in a purposeful and effective manner is essential to the entire counselling process, cultural factors can also play a major role. Working with Muslim clients often requires a culturally responsive approach that acknowledges the significance of their religious beliefs and practices. While basic knowledge of Islām can be enough in some cases, more advanced interventions often demand dual-domain expertise in both psychology and Islām.

It is important to recognise that even though manuals and standardised interventions can be effective for some clients, they might not be as suitable for others, like Mariam. In Mariam's case, simply applying what is found in the RCBT manual wouldn't have been effective and might have strained the therapeutic relationship from the onset. Equally important is that avoiding religion altogether would have been just as problematic. Thus, adapting to a religious context that is not straightforward requires flexibility and an understanding of the complexities involved. This showcases the need for specialised knowledge and a skilful approach that considers each client's unique circumstances. IMCBT can thus build on the utility of RCBT and provide additional benefits.

What IMCBT is also concerned with is not just the outcomes of the intervention that needs to be analysed but also the process or underlying mechanisms as well. That is, despite the overwhelming evidence to support both CBT and religiously integrated psychotherapy, it is important to keep a keen eye on why these interventions work and to uncover the underlying change mechanisms at the biological, cognitive, and affective bases of behaviour (see Hofmann & Hayes, 2019 for a deeper discussion on process-based therapy). Thus, as we deconstruct the evidence-based practice of CBT, we can begin to appreciate the nuances of what makes the therapy work for a specific client in a specific context and enhance existing RCBT manuals.

For example, in Chapter 14, we explored the use of *dua* or supplication interventions as a powerful tool to address an interpersonal conflict Malik has been having with his wife. The intervention was employed as a form of thought management and reframing, drawing upon Islāmic principles and connecting them to various clinical interventions and change mechanism processes. We explored the effectiveness of deepening our understanding of *dua* and its impact on thinking while providing Islāmic evidence supporting its use. One notable aspect discussed in this book is the understanding of negative self-talk as "waswasa" or whispers from the devil. Rather than attempting to change the client's interpretation of the source of these thoughts, we can use the advantageous approach of acknowledging them as spiritual challenges and intrusive thoughts simultaneously. By tapping into spiritual resources through the *dua* intervention, we can effectively facilitate cognitive interventions while maintaining fidelity to the principles of CBT, demonstrating how they can be seamlessly integrated and credible to both worldviews.

Beginning with the best in mind was another guiding principle used in the development of IMCBT and in my practice. In my opinion, one of the best ways to look at evidence-based practice is through adaptation and localisation or drawing on the generalities of the research while adapting to the unique characteristics of the individual (Norcross & Wampold, 2018). The Islāmic value that this principle is derived from is known as *Ihsan*. *Ihsan* is a spiritual state to strive in both being and doing. In essence, striving for *Ihsan* aspires to elevate ethical conduct to a higher spiritual level. It infuses everyday actions with consciousness of God's presence, creating a framework for upholding values that are both ethically sound and deeply rooted in faith. This principle transforms the mundane into the sacred, making every moment an opportunity to draw closer to our creator through ethical excellence. For example, despite confidentiality being a professionally regulated ethical requirement, we can extend this fundamental ethical principle to higher levels by recognising that to violate a client's right to confidentiality and anonymity, we may be in fact entering into the realm of hypocrisy from an Islāmic perspective. Although looking at the philosophical underpinnings is key to understanding a theory's development, in practice, the nomological net or rules that connect variables which are essential to demonstrate causality do not demonstrate that CBT practised by an atheist is more effective than the same one practised by a believer in God. On the contrary, adapting to the client's culture and religion using CBT techniques is what has been scientifically supported because it is about the client's beliefs, not the philosophical underpinnings nor the belief system of the therapist.

Rather, the belief system of the therapist may be considered a mediator for the therapeutic alliance when it is in line with that of the client. However, when it is not, it could lead to the perception (on behalf of the client) that the therapist may not understand them properly and lead to unseen factors causing ruptures in the relationship. Whether this assumption from the client is true or not is irrelevant; what matters is that the client perceives it to be true. Although time may be spent helping clients to challenge such misconceptions, it is more meaningful and respectful of the client and their time to provide them with an overview of how we will prioritise their preferences, culture, and religion.

Potential Application of IMCBT

Connolly and colleagues (2021) conducted a systematic review and meta-analysis on the use of lay counsellors providing mental health interventions. A "lay counsellor" is defined as a community member trained in mental health interventions without prior mental health expertise. Involving the community in health interventions is an underexplored approach with potential benefits. Utilising lay helpers is practical and critical. Existing evidence indicates their potential to address the surge in mental health needs, particularly in underserved communities. The global shortage of mental health services has been exacerbated by the COVID-19 pandemic, with increasing challenges expected in the post-pandemic era. According to the World Health Organization (WHO), the shortage of health workers across the developing world would reach about 18 million by 2030, thus demanding a practical solution. One such solution is to tap into existing community resources to alleviate the burden on healthcare professionals. They posited that providing laypeople in the community with professional training to provide mental health interventions would be an important endeavour. However, addressing this shortage is complex due to factors like cultural competence and limited training. However, according to the researchers, the missing piece is the concept of being professionally trained and thus lacking a coherent framework to work from.

If the critique of lay helpers is that they lack a coherent framework to work from and are thus not considered professionals, developing evidence-based practice frameworks that lay helpers can work from is both practical and critical; especially since many Muslims are already receiving support from these community helpers. Furthermore, ensuring such a framework is Islāmically based increases the likelihood of uptake making it acceptable to all parties, despite tensions between secular and Islāmic worldviews or those related to discourses around professionalism and training. IMCBT can be scaled to be delivered as a training manual for lay helpers and work towards the WHO's recommendation to enhance the surge capacity to address the surge of mental health needs around the world. IMCBT is intended to contribute to such a purpose. I hope you agree!

References

Abi Dawud (a). *Sunan Abi Dawud, 3660.* https://sunnah.com/abudawud:3660

Abi Dawud (b). *Sunan Abi Dawud, 366.* www.abuaminaelias.com/dailyHadīthonline/2019/07/05/cure-ignorance-ask-questions/

Abi Dawud (c). *Sunan Abi Dawud, 4993.* https://sunnah.com/abudawud:4993

Agilkaya-Sahin, Z. (2019). Have the Muslim psychologist left the lizard's hole? Developments in Islamic Psychology. *Turkish Studies*, *14*(2), 15–47. https://doi.org/10.7827/TurkishStudies.15018

Al-Jubouri, M. B., Isam, S. R., Hussein, S. M., & Machuca-Contreras, F. (2021). Recitation of Quran and music to reduce chemotherapy-induced anxiety among adult patients with cancer: A clinical trial. *Nursing Open*, *8*(4), 1606–1614. https://doi.org/10.1002/nop2.781

al-Tirmidhī (a). *Sunan al-Tirmidhī, 2988.* www.abuaminaelias.com/held-accountable-thoughts/

al-Tirmidhī (b). *Sunan al-Tirmidhī, 2518.* www.abuaminaelias.com/dailyHadīthonline/2012/08/18/leave-doubts/

al-Tirmidhī (c). *Sunan al-Tirmidhī, 3479.* www.abuaminaelias.com/dailyHadīthonline/2014/03/17/call-upon-allah-with-yaqin

al-Tirmidhī (d). *Sunan al-Tirmidhī, 2926.* https://sunnah.com/tirmidhi:2926

al-Tirmidhī (e). *Sunan al-Tirmidhī, 2002.* www.abuaminaelias.com/dailyHadīthonline/2012/03/31/good-character-heaviest-mizan/

al-Tirmidhī (f). *Sunan al-Tirmidhī, 2318.* www.abuaminaelias.com/dailyHadīthonline/2012/05/21/islam-perfection-not-concern-him/

American Psychological Association. (2020). *Education and training guidelines: A taxonomy for education and training in professional psychology health service specialties and subspecialties.* www.apa.org/ed/graduate/specialize/taxonomy.pdf

American Psychological Association, Presidential Task Force on Evidence-Based Practice. (2006). Evidence-based practice in Psychology. *American Psychologist*, *61*(4), 271–285.

Amole, M. C., Cyranowski, J. M., Conklin, L. R., Markowitz, J. C., Martin, S. E., & Swartz, H. A. (2017). Therapist use of specific and nonspecific strategies across two affect-focused psychotherapies for depression: Role of adherence monitoring. *Journal of Psychotherapy Integration*, *27*(3), 381–394. https://doi.org/10.1037/int0000039

APA. (2013). *Guidelines for the practice of telepsychology*. www.apa.org/practice/guidelines/Telepsychology
APA. (2021). *Apology to people of colour for APA's role in promoting, perpetuating, and failing to challenge racism, racial discrimination, and human hierarchy in U.S.* www.apa.org/about/policy/racism-apology
APA Dictionary. (n.d.(a)). *Neuroplasticity*. https://dictionary.apa.org/
APA Dictionary. (n.d.(b)). *Acceptance*. https://dictionary.apa.org/
Badri, M. (2007). *Contemplation: An Islamic psychospiritual study*. International Institute of Islamic Thought. https://doi.org/10.2307/j.ctvk8w1xc
Bandura, A., Ross, D., & Ross, S. A. (1961). Transmission of aggression through imitation of aggressive models. *Journal of Abnormal and Social Psychology*, *63*(3), 575–582.
Beach, R. A. (1993). *Teacher's introduction to reader-response theories*. Urbana, IL: National Council of Teachers of English.
Beck, A. T. (1967). *Depression: Clinical, experimental and theoretical aspects*. New York: Harper and Row.
Beck, A. T., & Dozois, D. J. (2011). Cognitive therapy: Current status and future directions. *Annual Review of Medicine*, *62*, 397–409. https://doi.org/10.1146/annurev-med-052209-100032
Beck, A. T., Emery, G., & Greenberg, R. (1985). *Anxiety disorders and phobias. A cognitive perspective* (pp. 300–368). New York: Basic Books.
Beck, A. T., Rush, A., Shaw, B., & Emery, G. (1979). *Cognitive therapy of depression*. New York: The Guilford Press.
Beck, J. S. (2021). *Cognitive behaviour therapy: Basics and beyond* (3rd ed.). New York: The Guilford Press.
Benish, S. G., Quintana, S., & Wampold, B. E. (2011). Culturally adapted psychotherapy and the legitimacy of myth: A direct-comparison meta-analysis. *Journal of Counselling Psychology*, *58*(3), 279–289. https://doi.org/10.1037/a0023626
Bowland, S., Edmond, T., & Fallot, R. D. (2012). Evaluation of a spiritually focused intervention with older trauma survivors. *Social Work*, *57*(1), 73–82. https://doi-org.cue.idm.oclc.org/10.1093/sw/swr001
Bukhârî (a). *Sahih Bukhârî, 71*. www.abuaminaelias.com/dailyHadīthonline/2011/08/20/if-allah-intends-good-fi qh/
Bukhârî (b). *Sahih Bukhârî, 127*. www.abuaminaelias.com/dailyHadīthonline/2019/04/08/ali-knowledge-narrate-understand
Bukhârî (c). *Sahih Bukhârî, 1303*. https://sunnah.com/Bukhârî:1303
Bukhârî (d). *Sahih Bukhârî, 6499*. https://sunnah.com/riyadussalihin:1
Bukhârî (e). *Sahih al-Bukhârî, 6136*. https://sunnah.com/Bukhârî:6136#
Bukhârî (f). *Sahih al-Bukhârî, 33*. www.abuaminaelias.com/dailyHadīthonline/2014/01/27/three-signs-of-hypocrite/
Bukhârî (g). *Sahih al-Bukhârî, 3037*. www.abuaminaelias.com/dailyHadīthonline/2011/02/12/allah-love-hate-servant/
Bukhârî (h). *Sahih al-Bukhârî, 13*. www.abuaminaelias.com/dailyHadīthonline/2011/03/18/love-brother-self/
Bukhârî (i). *Sahih al-Bukhârî, 6116*. www.abuaminaelias.com/dailyHadīthonline/2012/03/06/do-not-get-angry/

Bukhârî (j). *Sahih al-Bukhârî, 34.* www.abuaminaelias.com/dailyHadīthonline/2012/04/22/four-signs-nifaq/

Bukhârî (k). *Sahih al-Bukhârî, 3688.* https://sunnah.com/Bukhârî:3688

Campbell-Sills, L., Barlow, D. H., Brown, T. A., & Hofmann, S. G. (2006). Acceptability and suppression of negative emotion in anxiety and mood disorders. *Emotion, 6*(4), 587–595. https://doi.org/10.1037/1528-3542.6.4.587

Canadian Psychological Association. (2017). *Canadian code of ethics for psychologists* (4th ed.). Ottawa, ON: Author. https://cpa.ca/docs/File/Ethics/CPA_Code_2017_4thEd.pdf

Canda, E. R., & Furman, L. D. (2010). *Spiritual diversity in social work practice: The heart of helping* (2nd ed.). Oxford: Oxford University Press.

Captari, L. E., Hook, J. N., Hoyt, W. T., Davis, D. E., McElroy-Heltzel, S. E., & Worthington, E. L. (2018). Integrating clients' religion and spirituality within psychotherapy: A comprehensive meta-analysis. *Journal of Clinical Psychology, 74*(11), 1938–1951. https://doi.org/10.1002/jclp.22681

Chu, J., & Leino, A. (2017). Advancement in the maturing science of cultural adaptations of evidence-based interventions. *Journal of Consulting and Clinical Psychology, 85*(1), 45–57. https://doi.org/10.1037/ccp0000145

Ciarrocchi, J. W., Schechter, D., Pearce, M. J., & Koenig, H. G. (2014). *Religious cognitive behavioural therapy: 10-session treatment manual for depression in clients with chronic physical illness* (Christian version). https://spiritualityandhealth.duke.edu/index.php/religious-cbt-study/therapy-manuals/

Connolly, S. M., Vanchu-Orosco, M., Warner, J., Seidi, P. A., Edwards, J., Boath, E., & Irgens, A. C. (2021). Mental health interventions by lay counsellors: A systematic review and meta-analysis. *Bulletin of the World Health Organization, 99*(8), 572–582. https://doi.org/10.2471/BLT.20.269050

Cucchi, A. (2022). Integrating cognitive behavioural and Islamic principles in psychology and psychotherapy: A narrative review. *Journal of Religion and Health, 61*(6), 4849–4870. https://doi.org/10.1007/s10943-022-01576-8

Cuijpers, P., Miguel, C., Harrer, M., Plessen, C. Y., Ciharova, M., Ebert, D., & Karyotaki, E. (2023), Cognitive behaviour therapy vs. control conditions, other psychotherapies, pharmacotherapies and combined treatment for depression: A comprehensive meta-analysis including 409 trials with 52,702 patients. *World Psychiatry, 22*, 105–115. https://doi.org/10.1002/wps.21069

de Abreu Costa, M., & Moreira-Almeida, A. (2022). Religion-adapted cognitive behavioural therapy: A review and description of techniques. *Journal of Religion and Health, 61*(1), 443–466. https://doi.org/10.1007/s10943-021-01345-z

Deci, E. L., & Ryan, R. M. (1985). *Intrinsic motivation and self-determination in human behaviour*. Berlin: Springer Science & Business Media. https://doi.org/10.1007/978-1-4899-2271-7

Dobson, D., & Dobson, K. S. (2017). *Evidence-based practice of cognitive-behavioural therapy* (2nd ed.). New York: Guilford Press.

Easden, M. H., & Kazantzis, N. (2018). Case conceptualization research in cognitive behaviour therapy: A state of the science review. *Journal of Clinical Psychology, 74*(3), 356–384. https://doi.org/10.1002/jclp.22516

Ellis, A. (1980). Psychotherapy and atheistic values: A response to A. E. Bergin's "Psychotherapy and religious values." *Journal of Consulting and Clinical Psychology, 48*(5), 635–639. https://doi.org/10.1037/0022-006X.48.5.635

Eubanks, C. F., & Goldfried, M. R. (2019). A principle-based approach to psychotherapy integration. In J. C. Norcross & M. R. Goldfried (Eds.), *Handbook of psychotherapy integration* (pp. 88–104). Oxford: Oxford University Press. https://doi.org/10.1093/med-psych/9780190690465.003.0004

Flückiger, C., Del Re, A. C., Wampold, B. E., & Horvath, A. O. (2018). The alliance in adult psychotherapy: A meta-analytic synthesis. *Psychotherapy, 55*(4), 316–340. https://doi.org/10.1037/pst0000172

Fordham, B., Sugavanam, T., Edwards, K., Stallard, P., Howard, R., Das Nair, R., . . . Lamb, S. (2021). The evidence for cognitive behavioural therapy in any condition, population or context: A meta-review of systematic reviews and panoramic meta-analysis. *Psychological Medicine, 51*(1), 21–29. doi: 10.1017/S0033291720005292

Fouad, N. A., Grus, C. L., Hatcher, R. L., Kaslow, N. J., Hutchings, P. S., Madson, M. B., Collins, F. L., & Crossman, R. E. (2009). Competency benchmarks: A model for understanding and measuring competence in professional psychology across training levels. *Training and Education in Professional Psychology*, 3.

Fuertes, J. N., Spokane, A., & Holloway, L. (2012). *Specialty competencies in counselling psychology*. New York, NY: Oxford University Press.

García, O. (2009). *Bilingual education in the 21st century: A global perspective*. Oxford, UK: Wiley/Blackwell.

Gudykunst, W. B. (2005). An anxiety/uncertainty management (AUM) theory of strangers' intercultural adjustment. In W. B. Gudykunst (Ed.), *Theorizing about intercultural communication* (pp. 419–457). Thousand Oaks, CA: Sage Publications Ltd.

Hall, G., Ibaraki, A., Huang, E., Marti, C., & Stice, E. (2016). A meta-analysis of cultural adaptations of psychological interventions. *Behavior Therapy, 47*, 993–1014.

Haque, A., & Keshavarzi, H. (2014). Integrating indigenous healing methods in therapy: Muslim beliefs and practices. *International Journal of Culture and Mental Health, 7*(3), 297–314.

Haque, A., Khan, F., Keshavarzi, H., & Rothman, A. E. (2016). Integrating Islamic traditions in modern psychology: Research trends in last ten years. *Journal of Muslim Mental Health, 10*(1), 75–100.

Hayes, S. C. (2004). Acceptance and commitment therapy, relational frame theory, and the third wave of behavioral and cognitive therapies. *Behavior Therapy, 35*, 639–665. https://doi.org/10.1016/S0005-7894(04)80013-3

Hays, P. A. (2009). Integrating evidence-based practice, cognitive-behavior therapy, and multicultural therapy: Ten steps for culturally competent practice. *Professional Psychology: Research and Practice, 40*(4), 354–360. https://doi.org/10.1037/a0016250

Hays, P. A. (2016). *Addressing cultural complexities in practice: Assessment, diagnosis, and therapy* (3rd ed.). American Psychological Association. https://doi.org/10.1037/14801-000

Hebb, D. O. (1949). *The organisation of behaviour: A neuropsychological theory*. New York: Wiley & Sons.

Hodge, D. R. (2016). Spirituality, religion, and culture: Implications for social work practice. *Social Work, 61*(3), 197–205.

Hodge, D. R., & Nadir, A. (2008). Moving toward culturally competent practice with Muslims: Modifying cognitive therapy with Islamic tenets. *Social Work, 53*(1), 31–41. https://doi-org.cue.idm.oclc.org/10.1093/sw/53.1.31

Hofmann, S. G., & Hayes, S. C. (2019). The future of intervention science: Process-based therapy. *Clinical Psychological Science: A Journal of the Association for Psychological Science*, *7*(1), 37–50. https://doi.org/10.1177/2167702618772296

Husain, A., & Hodge, D. R. (2016). Islamically modified cognitive behavioural therapy: Enhancing outcomes by increasing the cultural congruence of cognitive behavioural therapy self-statements. *International Social Work, 59*(3), 393–405. https://doi-org.cue.idm.oclc.org/10.1177/0020872816629193

Ibn Kathir. (2000). *Tafsir ibn Kathir* (Trans. J. Abualrub, N. Khitab, H. Khitab, A., Walker, M. Al-Jibali, & S. Ayoub). Saudi Arabia: Darussalam Publishers and Distributors.

Ibn Mājah (a). *Sunan Ibn Majah, 4240*. www.abuaminaelias.com/dailyHadīthonline/2015/09/14/best-deeds-regular-small/

Ibn Mājah (b). *Sunan Ibn Majah, 79*. https://sunnah.com/ibnmajah:79#

Ibn Mājah (c). *Sunan Ibn Majah, 3657*. https://sunnah.com/ibnmajah/33

James, I. A. (2001). Schema therapy: The next generation, but should it carry a health warning? *Behavioural and Cognitive Psychotherapy*, *29*(4), 401–407. https://doi.org/10.1017/s1352465801004015

Kaplick, P. M., & Skinner, R. (2017). The evolving *Islam and Psychology* movement. *European Psychologist*, *22*(3), 198–204. https://doi.org/10.1027/1016-9040/a000297

Klepac, R. K., Ronan, G. F., Andrasik, F., Arnold, K. D., Belar, C. D., Berry, S. L., Christofff, K. A., Craighead, L. W., Dougher, M. J., Dowd, E. T., Herbert, J. D., McFarr, L. M., Rizvi, S. L., Sauer, E. M., Strauman, T. J., & Inter-organizational Task Force on Cognitive and Behavioral Psychology Doctoral Education. (2012). Guidelines for cognitive-behavioural training within doctoral psychology programs in the United States: Report of the Inter-Organizational Task Force on Cognitive and Behavioral Psychology Doctoral Education. *Behavior Therapy*, *43*(4), 687–697. https://doi.org/10.1016/j.beth.2012.05.002

Koenig, H. G., Pearce, M., Nelson, B., Shaw, S., Robins, C., Daher, N., Cohen, H. J., & King, M. B. (2016). Effects of religious vs. standard cognitive behavioural therapy on therapeutic alliance: A randomised clinical trial. *Psychotherapy Research: Journal of the Society for Psychotherapy Research*, *26*(3), 365–376. https://doi.org/10.1080/10503307.2015.1006156

Ledley, D. R., Marx, B. P., & Heimberg, R. G. (2010). *Making cognitive-behavioural therapy work* (2nd ed.). New York: Guilford.

Muslim (a). *Sahih Muslim, 2204*. www.abuaminaelias.com/dailyHadīthonline/2016/07/24/medicine-cure-allah-heal

Muslim (b). *Sahih Muslim, 2999*. www.abuaminaelias.com/everything-decreed-is-good-for-the-believer-both-ease-and-hardship/

Muslim (c). *Sahih Muslim, 2563a*. https://sunnah.com/muslim:2563a

Muslim (d). *Sahih Muslim, 144a*. https://sunnah.com/muslim:144a

Muslim (e). *Sahih Muslim, 1154*. www.abuaminaelias.com/dailyHadīthonline/2013/07/16/late-niyyah-voluntary-fast/

Muslim (f). *Sahih Muslim, 2732*. https://sunnah.com/muslim:2732a

Muslim (g). *Sahih Muslim, 2642*. www.abuaminaelias.com/dailyHadīthonline/2012/04/10/believers-praise-dunya/

Neenan, M., & Dryden, W. (2020). *Cognitive behaviour therapy* (3rd ed.). Taylor and Francis.

Norcross, J. C., & Goldfried, M. R. (Eds.). (2019). *Handbook of psychotherapy integration* (3rd ed.). Oxford: Oxford University Press. https://doi.org/10.1093/med-psych/9780190690465.001.0001

Norcross, J. C., Hogan, T. P., Koocher, G. P., & Maggio, L. A. (2016). *Clinician's guide to evidence-based practices: Behavioural health and addictions*. Oxford: Oxford University Press USA.

Norcross, J. C., & Karpiak, C. P. (2023). Relationship factors. In S. D. Miller, D. Chow, S. Malins, & M. A. Hubble (Eds.), *The field guide to better results: Evidence-based exercises to improve therapeutic effectiveness* (pp. 107–130). American Psychological Association. https://doi.org/10.1037/0000358-006

Norcross, J. C., & Wampold, B. E. (2018). A new therapy for each patient: Evidence-based relationships and responsiveness. *Journal of Clinical Psychology, 74*(11), 1889–1906. https://doi.org/10.1002/jclp.22678

Okajima, I., Komada, Y., & Inoue, Y. (2011). A meta-analysis on the treatment effectiveness of cognitive behavioural therapy for primary insomnia. *Sleep and Biological Rhythms*, 9, 24–34. https://doi.org/10.1111/j.1479-8425.2010.00481.x

Owens, J., Rassool, G. H., Bernstein, J., Latif, S., & Aboul-Enein, B. H. (2023). Interventions using the Qur'an to promote mental health: A systematic scoping review. *Journal of Mental Health, 32*(4), 842–862. https://doi.org/10.1080/09638237.2023.2232449

Paul, G. L. (1969). Behaviour modification research: Design and tactics. In C. M. Franks (Ed.), *Behaviour therapy: Appraisal and status* (pp. 29–62). London: McGraw-Hill.

Pavlov, I. P. (1927). *Conditioned reflexes: An investigation of the physiological activity of the cerebral cortex* (Trans. G. V. Anrep). London: Oxford University Press.

Piaget, J. (1952). *The origins of intelligence in children*. New York: International Universities.

Propst, R., Robins, C., Pearce, M., & Koenig, H. (2014). *Conventional cognitive behavioural therapy: 10-session treatment manual for depression in clients with chronic physical illness*. https://spiritualityandhealth.duke.edu/index.php/religious-cbt-study/therapy-manuals/

The Quranic Arabic Corpus. (2022). https://corpus.quran.com/qurandictionary.jsp?q=qbl

Rassool, G. H. (2021). *Islamic psychology: Human behaviour and experience from an Islamic perspective*. Routledge/Taylor & Francis Group. https://doi.org/10.4324/9780429354762

Rassool, G. H., & Khan, W. N. A. (2023). Hope in Islāmic psychotherapy. *Journal of Spirituality in Mental Health*, 1–15. doi: 10.1080/19349637.2023.2207751

Rathod, S., Gega, L., Degnan, A., et al. (2018). The current status of culturally adapted mental health interventions: A practice-focused review of meta-analyses. *Neuropsychiatric Disease and Treatment*, *14*, 165–178.

Rodolfa, E. R., Bent, R. J., Eisman, E. J., Nelson, P. D., Rehm, L. P., & Ritchie, P. L. (2005). A cube model for competency development: Implications for psychology educators and regulators. *Professional Psychology: Research and Practice*, *36*, 347–354.

Rønnestad, M. H., & Skovholt, T. M. (2003). The journey of the counsellor and therapist: Research findings and perspectives on professional development. *Journal of Career Development*, *30*(1), 5–44. https://doi.org/10.1023/a:1025173508081

Sabki, A., Sa'ari, C. Z., Muhsin, S. B., Kheng, G. L., Sulaiman, H., & Koenig, G. H. (2019). Islamic integrated cognitive behavior therapy: A Shari'ah-compliant intervention for Muslims with depression. *Malaysian Journal of Psychiatry*, *28*(1), 29–38.

Sarink, F. S. M., & García-Montes, J. M. (2023). Humor interventions in psychotherapy and their effect on levels of depression and anxiety in adult clients, a systematic review. *Frontiers in Psychiatry*, *13*, 1049476. https://doi.org/10.3389/fpsyt.2022.1049476

Scott, M. J. (2009). *Simply effective cognitive behaviour therapy*. Hove: Routledge.

Seedat, M. (2021). Signifying Islamic psychology as a paradigm: A decolonial move. *European Psychologist*, *26*(2), 131–141. https://doi.org/10.1027/1016-9040/a000408

Seekers Guidance. (2010). *Making 70 excuses for others in Islam: A key duty of brotherhood*. https://seekersguidance.org/articles/general-artices/making-70-excuses-for-others-in-islam-a-key-duty-of-brotherhood/

Seto, A., & Forth, N. L. A. (2020). What is known about bilingual counselling? A systematic review of the literature. *The Professional Counselor*, *10*(3), 393–405. https://doi.org/10.15241/as.10.3.393

Skinner, B. F. (1938). *The behaviour of organisms*. New York: Appleton-Century-Crofts.

Sue, D. W., Sue, D., Neville, H. A., & Smith, L. (2019). *Counselling the culturally diverse: Theory and practice* (8th ed.). Hoboken, New Jersey: Wiley.

Tanhan, A., & Young, J. S. (2022). Muslims and mental health services: A concept map and a theoretical framework. *Journal of Religion and Health*, *61*(1), 23–63. https://doi.org/10.1007/s10943-021-01324-4

Tompkins, J. P. (1980). *Reader-response criticism: From formalism to post-structuralism*. Baltimore: The Johns Hopkins University Press.

Trochim, P. W. M. K. (n.d.). *Knowledge base*. Knowledge Base – Research Methods Knowledge Base. https://conjointly.com/kb/

Twomey, C., O'Reilly, G., & Goldfried, M. R. (2023). Consensus on the perceived presence of transtheoretical principles of change in routine psychotherapy practice: A survey of clinicians and researchers. *Psychotherapy, 60(2)*, 219–224. https://doi.org/10.1037/pst0000489

Vansteenkiste, M. (2013, May). *Mustivation or motivation? The nurturing role of basic psychological need satisfaction.* Invited address at the Annual Meeting of the International Society for Behavioral Nutrition and Physical Activity, May 22–25, 2013, Ghent, Belgium.

Vroom, V. H. (1964). *Work and motivation.* San Francisco, CA: Jossey-Bass.

Walpole, S. C., McMillan, D., House, A., Cottrell, D., & Mir, G. (2013). Interventions for treating depression in Muslim patients: A systematic review. *Journal of Affective Disorders, 145*, 11–20. https://doi.org/10.1016/j.jad.2012.06.035

Watson, J. B., & Rayner, R. (1920). Conditioned emotional reactions. *Journal of Experimental Psychology, 3*(1), 1–14. https://doi.org/10.1037/h0069608

Weishaar, M. E. (1996). Developments in cognitive therapy. In W. Dryden (Ed.), *Developments in psychotherapy: Historical perspectives.* London: Sage.

Westbrook, D. (2014) The central pillars of CBT. In A. Whittington & N. Grey (Eds.), *How to become a more effective CBT therapist.* Chichester: Wiley.

Winch, G. (2013). *Emotional first aid: Healing, rejection, guilt, failure, and other everyday hurts.* New York: Plume.

Wood, J. V., Perunovic, E. W. Q., & Lee, J. W. (2009). Positive selfstatements. *Psychological Science, 20*(7), 860–866. https://doi.org/10.1111/j.1467-9280.2009.02370.x

Yalom, I. (2002). Religion and psychiatry. *American Journal of Psychotherapy, 56*(3), 301–316. https://doi.org/10.1176/appi.psychotherapy.2002.56.3.301

Yulish, N. E., Goldberg, S. B., Frost, N. D., Abbas, M., Oleen-Junk, N. A., Kring, M., Chin, M. Y., Raines, C. R., Soma, C. S., & Wampold, B. E. (2017). The importance of problem-focused treatments: A meta-analysis of anxiety treatments. *Psychotherapy (Chicago, Ill.), 54*(4), 321–338. https://doi.org/10.1037/pst0000144

Zulkifli, N., Zain, U., Hadi, A., Ismail, M., & Aziz, K. (2022). Effects of listening to Quran recitation and nature sounds on preoperative anxiety among patients undergoing surgery. *Pakistan Journal of Psychological Research, 37*(2), 295–310. https://doi.org/10.33824/pjpr.2022.37.2.18

Index